AF255225

Toward an American Renewal

Toward an American Renewal

Finding the Strength to Keep the Nation Together

ADAM M. BRODSKY

RESOURCE *Publications* · Eugene, Oregon

TOWARD AN AMERICAN RENEWAL
Finding the Strength to Keep the Nation Together

Resource Publications
An Imprint of Wipf and Stock Publishers
199 W. 8th Ave., Suite 3
Eugene, OR 97401

www.wipfandstock.com

PAPERBACK ISBN: 978-1-6667-7371-2
HARDCOVER ISBN: 978-1-6667-7372-9
EBOOK ISBN: 978-1-6667-7373-6

05/18/23

Translation of biblical passages reprinted from "The Koren Tanakh, Magerman Edition" with the permission of Koren Publishers Jerusalem Ltd.; and from "Tanakh: The Holy Scriptures" with the permission of The Jewish Publication Society, via https://www.sefaria.org/texts. Where noted, I have adapted the translation on my own.

Transliteration of biblical passages and Hebrew prayers provided by "Automatic Hebrew Transliteration," (https://alittlehebrew.com/transliterate/) using the "simplified modern Israeli" algorithm.

Selection of Robert Frost poem "The Road Not Taken" reprinted from the public domain.

הנה מה טוב ומה נעים שבת אחים גם יחד

Hinneh mah-tov umah-na'im shevet achim gam-yachad

How good and how pleasant it is to sit as brothers together.

—Psalms 133:1

Contents

Acknowledgments

I WOULD LIKE TO thank the many friends, teachers, and rabbis who took the time to review and edit my work. This project would not have been possible without their time and effort. Among them are Rabbi Yishai Fleischer; Rabbi Mike Feuer; Rabbi Yehuda Hakohen; Rabbi Michael Wasserman; Mr. David Don; Mr. Tom Spector; Mr. Rob McNutt; my parents, Dr. and Mrs. Ivan and Karen Brodsky; my eldest daughter, Lauren Brodsky; and of course my best friend, "עזר כנגדו—ezer kenegdo," and wife, Valerie Brodsky.

List of Abbreviations

AIPAC—American Israel Public Affairs Committee
b. B. Met.—Babylonian Talmud, Tractate Bava Metzia
Deut—Deuteronomy
ED—Emergency Department
Exod—Exodus
Gen—Genesis
Hos—Hosea
Lev—Leviticus
Isa—Isaiah
TBD—Theoretically Better Decision

In quoted Hebrew texts, the name of God is altered according to Jewish tradition in order to avoid reproducing the Hebrew name of God unnecessarily and out of respect for the Divine name. The Hebrew letter "ה—*Hey*" is replaced with the Hebrew letter "ק—*Kuf.*" Therefore the Tetragrammaton is rendered "יקוק" and the name "*Elohim*" is rendered "אלוקים—*Elokim.*"

The Tetragrammaton is transliterated as "*adonai*," which literally means "my master" and is used as a placeholder in keeping with Jewish tradition whereby the Tetragrammaton is never directly pronounced. It is rendered in English as "Lord."

Introduction

America today has social and political problems which go beyond simple polarization. Articles have been written and books published for at least the past twenty years lamenting the worsening polarization in American politics. However, in the post-Trump, post-capitol riots era of today one must ask, what is eating at the very fabric of our society? One must ask, how can it be that half the electorate believes the other to be illegitimate? Whether you believe in the correctness of the sentiment or not, how can it be that we have transitioned from lamenting our polarization but preaching unity, to suggesting that the other side be deprogrammed? How can it be that the talk in the shadows is of splitting the nation in two? What is at the root of this deepening sense of division in our society?

I am not a politician. I have never held public office. I am not a political science professor, nor am I a journalist, media personality, political philosopher, or social psychologist. I am a private citizen. I happen to work as a physician. I have grown up, lived, worked, and raised a family in the United States. I have lived in Minneapolis, Minnesota; St. Louis, Missouri; Boston, Massachusetts; Chicago, Illinois; and Phoenix, Arizona. Recently our family moved to Israel where we lived for a year and a half before moving back to the United States. Sometimes having some distance between one's self and a problem allows for a unique perspective, untainted by the gravity and inertia of vested interests, local political considerations, or career aspirations.

Over the past few years it has become clear to me that without some fundamental change our nation will most likely continue to become unglued. I am not free from bias and I claim no special authority with which to speak. But I do know that there needs to be an honest discussion in our country if we are to save ourselves. This short book simply contains my observations on the nature of the problems we face and what we can do to effect an American renewal.

At its root, the problem is more than polarization. It is more than people's opinions moving farther apart or becoming more extreme. Rather, it is related to the ferocity with which people cling to their own beliefs. It is the coupling of extremism with the notion that only I know what is best which drives the disunity and mistrust in our country. People of all stripes are unwilling to compromise because not only are they convinced that they alone are correct, but they are also convinced that if their exact plan is not adopted, the entire national project will fail utterly. It seems people therefore feel that the weight of the entire nation rests solely upon their shoulders and on the successful adoption of their platform. Under the stress of such a heavy load, how can anyone be expected to compromise?

It has been said many times that what we are lacking is civility; that disagreement, even deep, vigorous disagreement, is acceptable, but that the real problem we face is the inability to have civil discourse about our disagreements. Lack of civility, however, is not itself a foundational problem. Rather, it is merely a symptom of deeper, more elemental problems. Through the ensuing discussion of four specific yet foundational aspects of this problem, I hope to elucidate some of the reasons for the divisiveness, polarization, and lack of civility in our country and to highlight a possible way forward.

THE DEATH SPIRAL

In thinking of the situation in America today, I am reminded of a tragic yet well-known phenomenon in aviation known as the death spiral. Imagine a situation where I am piloting an aircraft. I am flying along normally in level flight and in smooth air but in the clouds such that I have no outside visual reference. I am therefore relying on my instruments to maintain straight and level flight. Imagine the plane is ever so slightly out of alignment such that if left alone with no input from the pilot the plane will tend to slowly bank left, similar to how a car which is out of alignment might constantly pull to the right or left unless actively held straight by the driver. If I am not careful and do not notice the plane slowly rolling to the left, the plane will eventually enter a leftward spiraling descent. Remember, the plane is in the clouds so I cannot tell just by looking out the window that the plane has become severely banked to the left. At some point I will notice two things on the instruments. First, I will notice the altitude suddenly going down very rapidly as the plane continues its spiraling descent. Second, I will notice on the attitude indicator (the instrument with the blue [sky] on top and the brown [ground] on the bottom, which by rolling freely is able to show the aircraft's position in space) that I am banked quite steeply to the left. Because the spiral was entered very slowly over some time, my sense of balance has acclimated to the spiral so that I don't feel it—to my senses it feels as if I am still flying straight and level.

I feel normal in this case, yet two instruments are showing the death spiral beginning to form: the attitude indicator showing the leftward bank and the altimeter showing the rapid descent. I will therefore attempt to correct these two conditions. First I will try to arrest the descent by pulling up on the yoke. Unfortunately, because the plane is so tightly banked, pulling back on the yoke only serves to tighten the turn making the death spiral even tighter and faster. (This occurs because pulling up on the yoke will pull the nose "up" only with respect to the direction the airplane is facing. When the aircraft is banked steeply such that the "top" of the airplane is actually facing sideways into the turn, then pulling up on the yoke will pull the nose of the plane in that sideways direction, more tightly into the turn.) Then, when I abruptly roll the plane in the opposite direction in an attempt to return to level flight, my sense of balance is suddenly confronted with a confusing situation. My senses feel as if they are turning the wrong way and there is an overwhelming sensation of spinning in the wrong direction. Remember, I felt straight and level when I was in the spiral such that any turn out of it will cause me to feel as if I am turning in the opposite direction. If I obey my senses (and not the instruments), I will turn the plane back into the spiral, until my sense of balance tells me that I feel level again.

Thus disoriented, I see myself rapidly descending toward the ground, all the while pulling up on the yoke as hard as I can which somehow seems to be making the situation worse and worse. It is as if the normal control inputs I have come to expect have all started working in reverse. In this case, the only way to break the spiral is to do the opposite of what I have learned, of what I have been doing up until that point. Namely, to stop pulling up in order to stop tightening the turn, to fight my own sense of balance—of what feels right—in order to truly level the plane, and only then to slowly climb out of the resulting straight and level dive.

Is America currently experiencing a kind of death spiral? Remember, the key points in the death spiral are that doing more of what you think is right only makes things worse, and you must fight against your own sense of orientation in order to regain control. As the extremist camps in our country sense our worsening situation, are they simply pulling on the yoke harder and harder, while to everyone's horror the situation only continues to worsen? Yet even as this occurs, every fiber of their being is telling them that they cannot let go, lest the whole country be lost. Their very strong sense of balance is so acclimated to the current death spiral that to move in any other direction simply feels horribly wrong, leading to nothing more than a frenzied paralysis as the country spirals perilously toward the ground. Perhaps the answer lies in relaxing one's grip on the yoke and doing the opposite of what "feels right" at the current moment. Perhaps only then will we be able to right our national ship.

THE CURRENT STATE OF ANALYSIS

If you watch the news, read the opinion sections of the major newspapers, or even search the internet looking for articles explaining the divisiveness in our country, you will find many explanations. First, there are articles dealing with the structural elements of politics in our country. These include articles about how the two party system lends itself to polarization as each party seeks to appear stronger, bolder, and more uncompromising. There are also articles about how the electoral primary system leaves the political parties beholden to their own most radical elements, as each candidate tries to outflank the others within the electoral constraints imposed by the fact that only the most extreme and politically invested members vote in the primaries. There are analyses about gerrymandered congressional districts resulting in so-called "safe seats" where the only opponent an incumbent is likely to face will come from the more extreme flank of his or her own party. All of these political explanations are no doubt true and do exert some influence, and yet they all seem inadequate to explain the full measure of the problem as we see it today. They seem academically correct and yet at the same time unsatisfying as full explanations. Each of those political realities has been long-standing for many years. What is different about today? Is it really the case that the political environment shapes the cultural norms? Or is it the other way around? Is society a reflection of politics, or politics a reflection of society?

Next, there are articles which are themselves partisan and which seek to explain the current polarized state of the country as the fault of the opposing political side. First in this category are articles lamenting the role of social media in furthering extremist agendas. Liberals are more likely to call for tougher restrictions on what they perceive to be political hate speech coming from the right, while conservatives are more likely to complain about the power to unilaterally censor speech being concentrated in the few silicon valley CEOs running the major social media platforms. While social media certainly does amplify divisions within our society, neither of these methods (conveniently supporting measures which in practice would simply block the other side's views from being heard or shared) are likely to contribute meaningfully to solving the overall issue of polarization and divisiveness in America today.

Then there are arguments which simply recapitulate long-standing partisan economic ideas. Thus on the Democratic side there are articles advocating for increased opportunities for the poor, better public school education, and increasing the minimum wage, as a way to reunite the country by better equalizing the opportunity for the American dream. Note, I am not saying that I disagree with any of these ideas, but those ideas are not specifically about reversing the polarization which plagues us. Rather, they are simply about doubling down on partisan political projects, no matter how correct they may be. There are also theories suggesting the rise of populism is to blame for the extremist tendencies we see today. Modern arguments against populism often make no attempt to disguise their partisan stance against the populism of the Republican party as led by former President Trump. Some go even further, suggesting that political parties today are too weak and decentralized to be able to control their own agendas. They long for a past when parties were controlled by strong-willed and knowledgable people who knew something about politics and good governance, and who could be counted on to do what was in the best interests of the country. Such strong parties would be insulated from the unstable populist power of demagogues. While this idea may contain some elements of truth, it runs the risk if carried to its logical conclusion of rule by an elitist oligarchy.

On the Republican side, calls to simply let government get out of the way which would allow everyone to have their shot at the American dream are similarly simply repeating standard Republican party planks in the guise of a remedy for divisiveness. At their most basic level, answers such as these all relate back to the unrealistic hope that if only the other side would come to their senses and join my side, then everyone would agree. But no matter how hard we may wish it to be so, that will never work.

These constitute the majority of the current explanations for the rise of extremism and polarization in America today: political structures, social media, populism, and economics. While each has an element of truth, I would argue that even taken together they are incomplete. I would further argue that each is only a symptom of deeper problems in our society. These deeper problems include how our culture socializes us to think about decision-making as well as certain aspects inherent to the unique nature of American society itself. I would therefore like to suggest four different solutions to the problems we face. These solutions operate at a much more basic level than the typical political or policy-oriented solutions which seem to be more common in government, media, and policy think-tank circles today. In that regard, they may appear at first to be unusual or at least different from what one would expect in more common discussions about American polarization. But I assure you, that is exactly the point. For when saying the same thing over and over again doesn't work, rather than reformulate the same tired platitudes, one must realize that an entirely new approach may be necessary.

THE SOLUTIONS

I have divided the solutions into two parts. The first part deals with how individuals and groups relate to each other. The second part deals with those forces which can act to maintain the unity of our country in opposition to the many divisive forces which have been accumulating over the past many years. The first part will begin by describing a theory of shared decision-making. This is important as it relates to the following foundational yet somewhat strange facet of democracy: in a democratic system everyone is expected to voice an opinion and yet only one opinion can ultimately become concrete action. The result is that most democratic participants spend the majority of their lives living with the uncomfortable discordance between their preferred opinion on any given issue and the decidedly different path which may have been ultimately chosen and with which they may stridently disagree. We will then expand on the notion of individual decision making to include group dynamics and certain responsibilities incumbent on the individuals within those various groups. The second part will begin by reorienting us to the special importance in the United States (as opposed to most other countries) of founding principals as an active force for unity. We will then end with a discussion of covenant as a framework through which to view the unity of our country.

It should be noted that none of these solutions are legal tweaks to the existing system, nor are they calls for legislative maneuvers whereby a simple majority vote in the House or Senate will be able to save our country from its current self-destructive path. Rather, they require new ways of thinking by individuals. They require a subtle cultural shift, personal reflection, and perhaps a different outlook on what it means to be part of this grand experiment called America. This may seem a tall order, but without each of us taking our measure of individual responsibility for the direction of the country, we risk the entire endeavor spinning out of control.

THE NATION OF ISRAEL

Throughout the ensuing discussions I will refer to examples from the Bible, the ancient Israelites, and Judaism to provide examples of how a successful nation is able to hold itself together over a span of millennia. This is not because reciting Biblical incantations has some magical power to bring supernatural goodness. It is simply because for the past three thousand years these ideas have successfully sustained the unity of the nation of Israel with its multiple incarnations stretching from the time of the Bible through the modern State of Israel. We should be able to learn from their experience and apply some of the lessons to our own modern country of America. It is no accident that the Bible was the guiding document which allowed the nation of Israel to adapt, survive, and grow through varied and challenging historical circumstances to this very day. The wisdom it contains therefore, whether you believe in religion, God, supernatural forces or not, has been empirically vetted in the only other idea-based nation to have survived longer than the United States of America. It is therefore worth understanding these lessons if we in America are to survive and heal ourselves today.

I realize that themes relating to religion, Israel, and the Bible may not speak to all in our country today. However, whatever we may think of those themes today, it is clear that at its founding and for many years after, our country's ethos had a biblical streak. From its founding America has been called the new promised land. We still end political speeches with, "God bless America," we still have "in God we trust" printed on our currency, and we still pledge allegiance to the "one nation, under God . . ." To the extent that this has been used to support one religion over another, or to the extent that it has been used by some in the past to support morally bankrupt positions, we must be ever-watchful. But as we know, the Bible has many interpretations. It is for us as a nation to decide what interpretations to bring to bear as it relates to our identity. I do not bring these "religious" discussions to light in order to convince you that the Bible should be treated as some kind of founding American document, nor that every American needs to be a Bible believer. But, as will be discussed in more detail in chapter 3, we in America are a very unique country given our purely idea-based beginning. Looking to guidance from another idea-based country seems like a reasonable approach, despite any current distaste for religion which some segments of modern society might harbor. Each of us, religious or not, can take those lessons and apply them to our own understanding of what it means to be an American.

Chapter One

Shared Decision-Making

LET'S BEGIN WITH SHARED decision-making. The type of shared decision-making I would like to discuss has three key components. The first is that it describes decisions which are made jointly by two or more people, as opposed to those made by a single individual or entity. The second is that it involves a framework whereby the same group of people or entities remain in relationship for an extended period of time, making several decisions together one after another. This is different than decisions among random groups of people where once the decision is made the group dissolves or changes so that no long-term relationship is established. The third is that the decision-makers have an express interest in maintaining the stability of their relationship into the future. For example, marriage partners make many decisions together and while they may disagree, they share an interest in maintaining the stability of their marriage. So too, political adversaries in any given country make political decisions, and at the same time each side has an interest in maintaining the stability of the country as a whole. That is different than decisions among superficial friends or acquaintances where if the disputes become too frequent or too fraught, the relationship can simply dissolve leaving the people in question free to form new or different relationships.

Healthy shared decision-making in this regard is not easy. There are two main spheres where this is typically operative. As described above, the first is family decision-making within a marriage, and the second is societal/political decision-making. In societal decision-making the specific individuals may change, however the groups involved often remain the same such that established relationship patterns are maintained which persist through time as multiple decisions are made within that relational framework. There are certainly other situations as well, such as workplace decisions, decisions among friends, peers, and siblings, or decisions between parents and children. All are interrelated and are subject to similar negative outcomes relating to disagreement: polarization, resentment, distrust, even hate. In order to have a successful shared decision-making experience we must keep the appropriate framework in mind.

Because the basic building block of society is the family, let us begin with a discussion of decision-making within the framework of marriage. For every decision which husband and wife jointly undertake there are four positions to consider. The first three are the easiest and most obvious. First, there is the wife's preferred course of action. Second, there is the husband's preferred course of action. Third, there is the actual course of action which stems from the joint decision process. This can be thought of as the outcome, the physical end result, or the path actually traversed by the couple. We'll call it the Actual Path. For simple decisions, the Actual Path may be exactly the husband's opinion or it may be exactly the wife's opinion. If the decision was whether to paint the bedroom blue or pink and after some argument the husband, who wants blue, relents to the wife's wish for pink, then the Actual Path (the room is painted pink) is the same as the wife's opinion. But in more complex decisions, it may not be quite so simple or obvious. Many decisions are not binary-type decisions with only two alternatives. In fact, most probably are not. In the above example, they could both agree to paint the room purple, a mix of blue and pink. Or they could begin painting it pink, then realize that given the lighting conditions the pink just doesn't look as good as the wife thought it would, so that they end up choosing a completely different color. The variations of what the Actual Path might look like are almost limitless and often do not resemble what either decision-maker had initially predicted.

These three positions—the husband's preferred course of action, the wife's preferred course of action, and the Actual Path—are easy and obvious. However it is the fourth position which ends up being the most important and which when left out leads to much of the polarization and anger which can be generated through disagreement in marriage and in society in general. That fourth position is, for lack of a better word, the "God's-eye view" of what the best possible decision would look like. If one believes in God then it can certainly be thought of as "what God would want," or "the decision that God would make." (In our example, would God choose blue or pink? Or maybe neither; maybe God prefers yellow?) However it in no way depends on belief in God. It is simply a theoretical construct about the best possible decision that could be made if one had access to unlimited data, which each decision-maker must concede might or might not agree with their own personal view. We'll call this the Theoretically Better Decision, or TBD. (If the abbreviation TBD reminds you of the phrase "to be determined," that is reasonable because the Theoretically Better Decision is never actually known; it always remains "to be determined.") This part is key and its importance cannot be overestimated. It is imperative that each person, in this example both the husband and the wife, accept the intellectual fact that there exists somewhere out there in space, somewhere in the universe, an unbiased TBD which would best serve the sum total of all the needs of the family, or whatever the current decision is about, and toward which they are both striving.

A THOUGHT EXPERIMENT

In order to better understand what this TBD represents, let us engage in the following thought experiment: Imagine an empty room. Now imagine four empty boxes in the room, arranged in two pairs; one pair for the wife and one pair for the husband. Into the first box of the husband's pair we are going to carefully place all of the information the husband has within his own mind about the current decision. All of the facts, all of the prior associations, all of the future predictions, all of the opinions, all of the logic, all of the previous experience, etc., which are contained within the husband's mind are going to be carefully placed into the first box. We will now do the exact same thing for the wife, again placing the entirety of the information which her mind contains about the current decision into the first box of her pair of boxes. At that point we have two pairs of boxes and in each pair there is one empty box and one box containing the relevant information about the current decision from each partner. If we were to craft an opinion, a decision, a recommended plan of action, out of the information within each of those boxes we would arrive at exactly the husband's or the wife's opinion.

We are now going to label the remaining two empty boxes "TBD," the theoretically better decision. There will be one TBD box for the husband and one TBD box for the wife. Let's proceed to the next step to see how this works. First, we are going to magically duplicate the contents of each of the first two boxes and place each duplicate into the empty TBD boxes. Now we have two identical "husband" boxes and two identical "wife" boxes, with each pair being an exact copy containing all of the relevant information that each one has about the decision at hand. For each pair of boxes, the first box is labeled "husband's opinion" or "wife's opinion," for out of the contents of those boxes we can fashion each one's exact opinion. The second box in each pair is labeled "TBD" although at this point it is still just a carbon copy of the first box.

This is where the fun begins. In the yard outside the room there is a well. However, this is not a well of water, rather, it is a well of infinite knowledge about the current decision. From this well we will gather buckets of additional knowledge, and we will pour this additional knowledge into each of the second boxes which are labeled TBD. Because these are magic boxes they have an unlimited capacity and therefore never overflow. Indeed, they are capable of holding all of the knowledge that we are pouring into them. We are going to continue adding information in equal quantities to both the husband's TBD box and to the wife's TBD box. The information we are adding to the two TBD boxes is the same relative to each other. For each bucket of extra information we give to the wife's box, we give an equal and identical bucket to the husband's box, and we are going to continue adding this extra information forever.

As we are doing this, if at any point we were to temporarily stop in order to craft an opinion out of either TBD box, it would contain more information than the corresponding original "husband's opinion" box or "wife's opinion" box, which have remained constant from the point at which they were filled with the original information from the minds of each spouse. Therefore, that newly crafted plan of action out of either TBD box would be a better plan of action than the original, since it is derived from more information. As time goes on and the TBD boxes become filled with more and more information, the decisions which may be crafted from them also become better and better. Furthermore, note what happens to the TBD boxes relative to each other. At first they appear to be different. They are, after all, carbon copies of the husband's and the wife's initial knowledge base and opinions, which are not the same. However, as we continue to add more information to each, in equal proportions and of equal content, they begin to resemble each other more and more.

If we consider time to stretch forward in a never ending line, we can add to our thought experiment a time dimension. As we look forward in time, we will see all of the future iterations of the two TBD boxes being continuously filled with more and more knowledge, stretching on into the distance toward the infinite future. If we squint our eyes, peering ahead toward that infinite time horizon, we will begin to notice the outline of a figure. It is difficult to make out exactly who or what they are, being so far away, but they are stationed exactly at the infinite time horizon. In fact, they are patiently waiting to collect and inspect the final TBD boxes after we have finished adding all of the infinite information to each one. The title of this figure is the Great Overseer of Delivery because they are waiting for the final delivery of the two TBD boxes. We can abbreviate their title G.O.D. After we have been doing this for, say, an entire year, or maybe an entire lifetime, pouring bucket after bucket of new knowledge into each box, the original "different" information with which each box started will make up only a tiny fraction of the total information in each box, and the two boxes will therefore become more and more alike. Why? Because by that time most of the total information in each box will be comprised of the newly added information which is the same for each box. All of the newly added information will essentially dilute out the original information, bringing the contents of the two boxes closer and closer together.

As we continue this experiment forward in time, the character of the information in the two TBD boxes will asymptotically approach each other, never becoming exactly equal yet continuously moving closer and closer together, forever, as they approach the G.O.D. As the two TBDs (Theoretically Better Decisions) which may be crafted from the contents of each TBD box become better and better, as we move forward in time toward infinity, they will tend to converge toward a single point, right where the G.O.D. stands ready to receive them. From the G.O.D.'s perspective, standing at infinity, the two boxes have by that time begun to converge. That asymptotically-merged TBD box which comes from the convergence of the two spouse's TBD boxes is what the G.O.D. finally receives. When the G.O.D. takes receipt of the two converged TBD boxes, the G.O.D. will craft another opinion, another plan of action, another decision. This decision, formed at the point of infinity, at the point of infinite knowledge, by the G.O.D, is the best decision which can be rendered.

It is also worth noting that the decision which the G.O.D. crafts from the convergence of the TBD boxes is not a simple average of the opinions crafted from the two original boxes. Why not? Because we do not know the contents of the well of knowledge. We do not know the nature of the information that we are adding to each box. If we consider decisions or opinions to be represented in our model by points in space, then unlike parallel lines which appear to converge to a point exactly midway between the two lines, in our example we are not sure of the exact location of the final point of convergence. It could be somewhere in the middle, but it is equally likely that the two boxes end up converging to a point far away to one side or the other.

This thought experiment shows us what this Theoretically Better Decision, the TBD, represents. It shows us that despite the fact that each party, in this case the husband and wife, begins with differing opinions due to different knowledge bases, that if they could increase their knowledge base infinitely, each one's opinion would continue to become more and more refined until they would begin to converge in the end. Remember, this is only a thought experiment, not what happens in real life. But it does illuminate for us the point toward which each one is striving. Each person is aware that they are trying as best they can to arrive at that converged TBD. However, because the actual converged TBD cannot be known, we will never know in the present if either the husband's or the wife's position is the same as that TBD. Similarly, we will never even know who's decision is closer to the TBD. All we know is that we have the husband's decision, the wife's decision, the converged TBD, and the Actual Path taken.

If you don't like the "God's-eye view" terminology or the multiple boxes thought experiment to describe the TBD, we can describe it using more familiar modern science. In medicine when we study a new drug or new treatment we do a series of randomized controlled trials often involving many thousands of patients in order to determine if the new medication or treatment works as expected. Even so, we are never 100 percent certain that the treatment works and sometimes many years later new data emerges refuting the earlier data. In the realm of marital, social, and political decision-making such data does not exist. Let's take the tax code as an example. One might engage in another thought experiment where one would create thousands of "Americas" and in each one apply a different tax code. In some we would tax the wealthy more, in some we would apply an even flat tax, in some we would equalize the capital gains tax, corporate tax, individual income tax, etc. We would simply repeat these experiments thousands of times until it became clear which tax policy resulted in the most equitable and successful social and economic results. This would be the TBD. The problem is obviously that we don't have access to such experiments. We may have computerized economic models and simulated experiments, but everyone knows that these simulations never account for all the variables operative in real life. Thus the best we can do is make educated guesses. In our example of the husband and wife deciding which color to paint the bedroom, it would be nice if we could create thousands of experimental families where some grew up with blue bedrooms, some with pink bedrooms, and then we observed them to see which families had better outcomes while holding all other variables constant. Alas, we do not have access to such data. Therefore the husband and wife must make educated guesses. From a scientific standpoint, the TBD is the decision we would reach if we had access to an unlimited amount of data. In the absence of such data, both the husband and the wife form their own opinions utilizing their own incomplete data sets, each attempting to arrive as closely as possible to that TBD.

So far, this schema doesn't help the intimate mechanics of doing what must be done: of choosing a course of action in the present. That must still be negotiated as carefully as possible. The husband and wife do the best they can through argument, debate, stamping their feet up and down, and somehow what emerges will be the Actual Path. It will be either a compromise midway between the two positions, or one will be convinced, or some other piece of information will be obtained pulling in one direction or the other, or one path will be chosen initially which will yield a dead end causing an unexpected change, or some unexpected turn of events will occur making one path easier, or possibly new information will cause it to diverge down another unanticipated path. For example, maybe they decide to go with pink but when they get to the paint store they find that there has been a run on pink. Maybe they also find that due to a massive glut of blue, the blue paint is much cheaper and comes with a lifetime warranty. That new information may change the decision even after it has been made initially. It is important to remember that the ultimate path traversed, the Actual Path, may not be the exact decision for which either decision-maker had initially hoped. But the knowledge that the path each had hoped for may not be the TBD anyway makes the journey down the Actual Path more tolerable. For perhaps the Actual Path will be closer to the TBD than either of the decision-maker's initial opinions.

MULTIPLE DECISIONS

Perhaps our example of just one simple decision is too unrealistic. Let's consider a series of decisions since that's really what life is about, and let's try to inhabit the mind of one of the decision-makers, say the husband. He knows what he wants, he knows what his wife wants, and he knows that they each want something different; they disagree. He also knows that a TBD is out there somewhere, but he doesn't know what that is exactly. He of course thinks his position is closer to that TBD than is his wife's position. That's almost the definition of what it means for him to make a decision or have an opinion. We are always trying to do what is right—what is closest to the TBD. However, in considering, say, the last ten decisions that the couple has made together or the next ten decisions they will make in the future, in each and every case the TBD could be closer to his position or closer to his wife's position. It immediately becomes clear that unless he is a prophet receiving divine revelation, the chances that in all ten cases his decision will be closer than hers to the TBD are quite small. It would be like flipping a coin ten times and getting heads each and every time. While possible, it is very unlikely.

Why is this so? Maybe he thinks that he is smarter or better suited to decision-making or has a world outlook that makes his decision-making consistently better, consistently closer to the TBD? Here he must realize that part of what makes the TBD the better decision is that it is made by taking into account all possible information, something which he will never have. But if his decision is wrong, i.e., not the TBD, are we saying that his decision-making process is somehow flawed? Are we not accusing him of making an error? Yet what if he has carefully gone over his decision and made sure that there are no errors? How do we reconcile the fact that he has not made any errors and yet he may not have arrived at the TBD?

The answer is that he must realize not that his decision-making is somehow inherently flawed, but rather that the sum total of information available to any one individual is simply incomplete. Not only that, but the sum total of decision-making biases which he harbors internally are specific to his set of life experiences. While he can indeed be very smart, even capable of making the best decisions possible given the information to which he has access, his decisions are still limited by the set of information which he is able to amass about the decision and by the innate biases, beliefs, and opinions which he internally holds and which he cannot control. Once he recognizes this he will immediately see that the exact same thing is occurring with respect to his wife—that the sum total of information which she is able to amass is different for her than for him, and the sum total of her internal biases, beliefs, and opinions, are different than his (and equally uncontrollable by her). He further must realize that the TBD by definition is not bounded by any of that. That's why it's the TBD. Recall from our previous thought experiment that the TBD includes an infinite amount of information. The TBD, far from being free of biases, on the contrary actually takes into account all possible biases. It is indeed made up of the summation of an infinite amount of internal biases, beliefs, and opinions. While he may feel that his position is closer than hers to the TBD, he also knows from his high school mathematics class that the distance between any two different points and infinity is exactly the same—infinity. Thus he knows, at least mathematically, that the distance between his position and the TBD is exactly the same as the distance between his wife's position and the TBD—they are both infinity.

If that seems strange, remember that the TBD is made up of an infinite amount of information, while both his and his wife's are made up of only a finite amount of information. It may be more precise to say that the amount of information that goes into the TBD is infinitely more than the amount of information that went into either the husband's or the wife's decision. Because we can assume that the more information one has about a decision the better the ultimate decision will be, the two situations end up being approximately equal. Thus if the amount of information that went into the decision was infinitely more for the TBD than it was for either the husband's or the wife's decisions, then the ultimate correctness or effectiveness of the decision itself would also be infinitely better than either the husband's or the wife's decision.

With this knowledge, he comes to expect that the Actual Path taken, wishing as he does for it to be as close as possible to the TBD, indeed should not line up every time either with his position or with his wife's position. The simple law of averages tells how incredibly improbable it would be for it to line up exactly with his position every time. In fact, this rule is so iron-clad that if one were to find a situation where the decisions made were in fact always in accordance with only one party's view, it would be extremely suspicious and appear to be a result of coercion rather than shared decision-making.

THE AMERICAN MARRIAGE

So far we have been discussing decision-making within the confines of marriage. Below we will broaden the scope to include larger groups, political parties, and the entire country in general. But before we do, it is worth dwelling on the marriage construct a little longer. The family unit is the basic unit of our society. It is within the context of the family that we raise our children and therefore the future generations of our country depend a great deal on the success of the family structure. As a new generation of young adults reaches maturity, their skill set relating to interpersonal relationships, coping with disagreement, and conflict management will be greatly influenced by what they observe, consciously or unconsciously, during their formative years at home.

Therefore, its importance cannot be overstated. One of the keys to improving political dialogue and polarization in our society as a whole is to improve dialogue at its most basic level, between husband and wife. If successful, this will effect a reduction of the current divisiveness in politics and will cause the next generation of Americans to be less divisive themselves.

Because in our current political environment even benign sounding words have become polarized, I want to make a disclaimer before continuing. I want to be very clear that when I speak about family I do not mean to push any political agenda. I do not say the word "family" in order to include or exclude anybody. Specifically, I am not speaking for or against any particular definition of marriage. For the purposes of this discussion, its exact definition does not matter. What matters is the relationship between the participants. I have been using the terminology "husband and wife" simply because it is the most commonly used terminology but I do not mean to exclude anybody who feels this definition to be in any way restrictive. That is not to say that one could not have such a discussion, but simply that this book is not the place for it. The concepts in this book related to marriage are universal, no matter what position you take on its definition.

I would like to start with a brief thumbnail sketch of an idealized American marriage. Many young, unmarried people, when asked to imagine the perfect marriage, would likely hold two images in their mind. First, they would think about their parents' marriage, likely imperfect and perhaps in their young eyes not worth emulating, or at least necessitating some improvements. Second, they would probably have a beautiful Hollywood image in their mind of a perfect marriage; one where the two young people fall madly in love with each other, enjoy a robust romantic and sexual life together, pursue common interests, and almost can't believe how they magically seem to like the same quirky music that no-one else seems to get into, the same cuisine, the same philosophizing about life's big questions, and generally seem to agree on most everything as if it were written in the stars that they were meant for each other. This view of marriage is quite common, is portrayed time and again in novels, television shows, and movies and strikes a deep chord with the American psyche. But I would like to contrast this view with a view taken from the repository of Israelite and Jewish tradition, the Bible.

Now don't worry, this has nothing to do with sexism or chauvinism or some quaint nostalgia for the way things "used to be." Rather, this has to do specifically with the way the husband and wife are supposed to ideally relate to each other within the marriage. Nor does this have to do with creationism or evolution or any other sort of childish biblical literalism. Whether you take the biblical stories literally or allegorically, in either case they have much to teach us about the ancient wisdom of the Israelites and their progeny, Judaism and the modern State of Israel. Indeed, one could even make a case for including all of Christianity and Islam within the realm of the religious "progeny" of the Bible. Therefore, whether you are a "Bible believer" or not, it is a worthwhile endeavor to attempt to understand its messages.

Relating to our discussion of marriage, there are two biblical verses which deserve our attention. Their context is the story of the creation of Adam and Eve, the paradigmatic first marriage. In the story Adam is created first, followed by Eve. There is an interesting verbal motif which is repeated twice when describing the reason why it was necessary to create Eve. Please keep in mind, this is not some misogynistic rant about how the male was created first and was then lucky enough to be granted a female for his pleasure. One must note that during the short period of time when Adam existed before the creation of Eve, the Bible does not refer to Adam ever as "him" or in any other way hint that Adam was necessarily a male, one half of a gendered species as we know males today. A better question to ask, rather than why was Eve created, is why was it not enough to simply have a single (androgynous?) human (Adam) with unisex progeny? Why was it necessary for the first person, Adam, to be split (almost literally/surgically, as the story goes) into a male Adam and a female Eve? The first verse to comment on this question is Gen 2:18:

ויאמר יקוק אלקים לא טוב היות האדם לבדו אעשה לו עזר
כנגדו

*Vayyomer adonai elohim lo-tov heyot ha'adam levaddo
e'eseh-lo ezer kenegdo.*

The LORD God said, "It is not good for the human to be
alone; I will make a fitting helper for him."[1]

In the next verse God brings all the animals before the human in
order that the human choose a name for each animal. The very
next verse repeats the same phrase, "fitting helper," once again as it
becomes clear that, apparently in contrast to the animals, there is
no counterpart for the human (Gen 2:20):

ויקרא האדם שמות לכל הבהמה ולעוף השמים ולכל חית השדה
ולאדם לא מצא עזר כנגדו

*Vayyikra ha'adam shemot lechol-habbehemah ule'of ha-
shamayim ulechol chayyat hassadeh ule'adam lo-matza
ezer kenegdo.*

And the human gave names to all the cattle and to the
birds of the sky and to all the wild beasts; but for the human no fitting helper was found.[2]

The phrase "עזר כנגדו—*ezer kenegdo*—fitting helper" stands out
first because of the somewhat awkward repetition. The text already
established, in none other than the voice of God, God's plan to
make a fitting helper for the human. Then, as if a friend is telling a
story and suddenly can't remember if they forgot to mention some
piece of vital information, the text says again that no fitting helper
was found. But we already know that—not only do we already
know that, but this wasn't some random person telling us a story,
it was God God's self, who presumably doesn't make mistakes. So
why the repetition?

1. Translation adapted from *Tanakh: The Holy Scriptures.*
2. Translation adapted from *Tanakh: The Holy Scriptures.*

Second, the actual words used are not what they appear. If we look at the Hebrew "עֵזֶר כְּנֶגְדּוֹ—*ezer kenegdo*," fitting helper is not an adequate translation. It is true that the word עֵזֶר—*ezer* does mean "help" or "helper." But the second word, כְּנֶגְדּוֹ—*kenegdo* does not mean "fitting." The root of the word, נגד—*neged*, actually means "against." There are other words in Hebrew which mean "to fit," in the sense of complementarity or appropriateness, but those words are not used. There is also another Hebrew word which means "opposite" in the more neutral sense of "across from" or "in front of," however that word was not used either. The specific word used here, "נגד—*neged*—against," has a distinctively negative connotation. For example, the modern Hebrew word for "antibodies" is נוגדנים—*nogdanim*, from the same root, because antibodies are little molecules which work specifically against something, in that case viruses. Therefore, a more accurate translation would be, "I will make a helper against him," for the first verse, and "but for the human, there was not found a helper against him." What is the text hinting at with the repetition of this seemingly negative phrase? Shouldn't the husband and wife be working together? Why should one spouse be "against" the other spouse?

MARRIAGE REEXAMINED

Let us reexamine the idealized American marriage we postulated earlier; the one where the husband and wife magically seem to share a host of common interests and lovingly agree on everything. Most people realize that this is only a stylized ideal and that in practice most marriages are not like that. Most people realize that even the best marriages have their share of disagreements. Most people realize that despite these disagreements, we must do the best we can to respect our spouse, to try to understand each other, to always remember that we love each other and that we both want what is best even when we disagree. But even in this perhaps more realistic view of marriage, the disagreements which inevitably creep into the relationship are usually seen as unfortunate obstacles to the loving union which marriage is supposed to embody. In this view the disagreements are challenges to be overcome. They are bumps on the road of life. It is simply the unfortunate reality that relationships, even the marriage relationship, cannot be perfect. What we now see instead is that the biblical text is telling us that this idealized view is exactly backwards. When the text repeats the phrase "against him," it is hinting at one of the main functions of marriage. It is telling us that far from disagreements being incidental to marriage or problems to be swept aside which prevent us from actualizing the ideal (problem-free) marriage we all want, disagreements are in fact integral to marriage. Indeed, one might even say they are the whole point of marriage. The biblical text tells us that the appropriate relationship between spouses is that they stand "against" each other.

If we return to our discussion of shared decision-making between marriage partners, we now see that our model does not simply describe how we can best deal with our imperfect human proclivity for disagreement. Rather, it is a model which describes how it is exactly through our relationships with different people with different opinions, both in marriage and in the broader sociopolitical context as a whole, that we are able to find our way towards the TBD. Far from being a means to simply minimize some random evil inherent in our frail human condition, it is a necessary and purposeful component of our very existence. It is only through argument and debate, the push and pull of the marriage partners acting "against" one another, that the Actual Path ends up being as close as possible to the TBD. Recognizing this, we are able to "up our game," as it were, maximizing our potential to find the TBD in every facet of our lives in a way which could never occur were it not specifically for our spouse, our friends, or even our political adversaries, standing "against us."

GAMING THE SYSTEM

This would be a good time to point out how it is possible for a cynic to "game the system." If the husband knows that the TBD (and therefore hopefully the Actual Path) is statistically going to be sometimes closer to his position and sometimes closer to his wife's position, and if over time he wants to move the Actual Path closer to his own position, he may think that by artificially making his position more extreme he can pull the "average" Actual Path closer to what his true position was initially. Our model of shared decision-making assumes that each party is honest about their beliefs and that they advocate for what they really believe to be true. It is the hope that widening one's view to see the entire picture, specifically including the fact that the TBD is unknown, will help people avoid the temptation to game the system. The success of the entire system rests exactly on the avoidance of such temptation. If this is difficult, and indeed it may be, at least by understanding the larger picture people can begin to more actively decide how they wish to behave, rather than leaving it to their subconscious or to instinct. In the end, the success or failure of society rests on the thoughts and actions of individuals.

This may seem a bit too much like simple moralizing, as if the success or failure of the entire endeavor boils down to telling everyone to just be honest. You may say to yourself that's too obvious, everyone knows that already but it never works and that's why it can't be the lynchpin of any plan to help America renew itself. You may say that just asking people to behave morally is a bridge too far; that in America there is no expectation that people act morally or honestly, just legally. I would remind you, then, of the massive stock market fluctuations involving Gamestop and AMC Theaters in early 2021.[3] I am not a financial expert but the basic problem in that case was that the fundamentals of the stock market broke down because many people at the same time tried to game the system. (Briefly, hedge funds were planning to short-sell the stock of these companies which were doing poorly due to a combination of market conditions, the COVID-19 pandemic, etc., when thousands of individual internet investors linked via social media bought shares of these companies at the same time with the intent of artificially raising the price in order to financially harm the short-selling hedge funds. The scheme worked, causing

3. Hirtenstein, "AMC, GameStop Swing."

massive price fluctuations, a lot of market consternation, large financial losses to some and gains to others.) In other words, the stock market, which is a fundamental part of the American capitalist system, relies on all participants buying and selling shares of companies honestly in order to effect real valuations of those companies based on market expectations. When the market, made up of individual people each acting in their own honest interest, functions well, its function of moving capital efficiently to companies which are in the best position to utilize that capital, works well. There is an expectation that people will act honestly. Sure, there are short-sellers and speculators who may deviate from this pattern, but if the market is big enough it can handle a certain percentage of that "dishonest" behavior without collapsing. However, when enough people begin acting dishonestly at the same time, the market ceases to function. The fact that people are expected to act "normally" (honestly) is not considered weird or too obvious or just a bunch of moralizing nonsense; on the contrary, it's the only way the market can function. Our interactions as we collectively make decisions are no different.

THE OVEN OF ACHNAI

Getting back to our decision-making theory, I would like to point out that the most important part of this theory is the recognition that there exists a TBD which is always unknowable and is likely to be different from the opinion of either you or your adversary. To illustrate how important it is that the TBD remain unknowable, I would like to share a story from the Talmud, the Jewish compendium of legal debates, arguments, and commentary. In the talmudic story of the oven of Achnai[4] which takes place approximately 1700 years ago, a group of rabbis were engaged in debate about a point of law relating to the susceptibility to ritual impurity of a certain type of oven. All of the rabbis agreed except for one lone holdout who refused to concede. This one particular

4. b. B. Met. 59b.

rabbi felt absolutely convinced that he was correct and that the rest of the rabbis were simply not understanding or perhaps not even capable of understanding the correctness of his position. In exasperation he cried out, "If I am right, the carob tree will prove it," and lo and behold, the carob tree immediately jumped up and moved one hundred cubits away. The other rabbis said, "Legal decisions are not decided by carob trees." He then said, "If I am correct the stream will prove it," and the waters of the stream immediately began to flow backwards. But the rabbis said, "We do not learn legal decisions from streams." The rabbi then said, "If the law is according to my opinion let the walls of the study hall prove it," and immediately the walls of the study hall began to collapse. One of the other rabbis rebuked the walls causing them to steady themselves. Finally, he cried out, "if my opinion is correct the heavens will prove it," whereupon a heavenly voice which was heard by the entire group answered that indeed he was correct, and the law was meant to be according to his opinion. The other rabbis, instead of bowing before the heavenly voice and accepting the decree, made the audacious statement, "The Torah is not in heaven," meaning that the Torah, the book of Jewish law, was given by God to humanity and decisions here on earth are made here on earth in accordance with the majority rabbinic opinion. Indeed, they excommunicated the dissenting rabbi and stood by their communal decision, different as it was from the "wishes" of the heavenly voice. They didn't want to have all legal decisions made unilaterally by someone who "knows" they are right all the time because they have access to a heavenly voice and therefore can't be part of the general deliberations.

How strange this is. How could it be that when God makes God's decision known, that the rabbis could refuse to follow it? Placing this story in the framework of our above discussion, this is because while the TBD (the heavenly voice in the talmudic story) indeed represents the most correct decision, it must by definition remain unknowable. It is only useful insofar as we know that it theoretically exists and that it defines the direction towards which we are striving. However, the minute it becomes known (again, the heavenly voice actually talking to the rabbis) it loses its significance. It either devolves into just another person's opinion, because many people can claim to speak in the name of God, or if all present agree that it really was a voice from heaven then it gums up the whole process and renders the entire exercise, indeed all of existence, moot by effectively depriving people of free choice.

MODERN POP CULTURE

Lest you think that this concept is restricted to esoteric talmudic discussions, I would like to briefly highlight two modern science fiction films which hinge upon the same concept—that the TBD must remain unknown. The first is a movie called *Gattica*.[5] This movie takes place in a future where gene sequencing has become commonplace to the extent that one is able to predict with a high degree of accuracy not only the probability of future disease states but also human capacities such as emotional stability, drive, ambition, etc. In this world society has switched from racial profiling and discrimination to genetic profiling and discrimination. This has resulted in an upper class with the right genes who are employed in sought-after, high-paying jobs, and an underclass of those with less desirable genes who simply do menial labor. This social order is maintained because in this society no high-end company would want to waste its time and resources on someone who was genetically destined to fail. One can immediately see the discomfort with this imagined dystopian future. While on the one hand, it seems perfectly reasonable to expect that people would be matched to the professions in which they are genetically destined to excel; on the other hand, it robs society of free will by simply herding entire classes of people one way or the other based on the predictive knowledge of their genetic composition. While we all desire more information as a general rule, we shudder at the thought of too much information rendering our own individual decision-making capacity obsolete. We prefer that each have the

5. Niccol, *Gattica*.

ability to try as best they can to reach their own goals and make their own decisions. In this sense we want our ultimate genetic destiny to remain unknown, akin to the TBD in our earlier discussion. Once it becomes known, as the movie portrays, it devolves into a creepy, Orwellian albatross hanging around our necks at every turn.

The second movie to which I would draw your attention is Minority Report,[6] another futuristic dystopian science fiction film. The premise in this film is that human evolution has progressed to a point where a few individuals are able to read the minds of others, predicting what they are about to do. A technologically advanced apparatus has been constructed which can harness and amplify the predictive power of these individuals to scan the population for nefarious activity. Computer algorithms can then predict with near-certainty if a person is about to commit a crime before they have actually carried out the action. At that point the police are dispatched and the person is arrested for the crime they were about to commit. This is seen as a breakthrough because it allows law enforcement to be proactive rather than reactive, preventing crimes such as murder before they occur. Without this technology, law enforcement would have been alerted after the fact, once the victim had already been murdered. And yet, here too, the creepiness is unavoidable. Despite the advance in knowledge which seems to be able to prevent crime, it seems unbearably unfair to arrest people for crimes which they have not yet actually committed. Free will seems to be jettisoned entirely when waiting for someone to make their own choice becomes obsolete in the face of superior knowledge. The premise of the movie again rests on the foundation that too much knowledge is not always a good thing, that some knowledge, like our TBD, is better left unknown.

In both of these movies, more knowledge carries the possibility of arriving at better, more accurate decisions which can enhance societal outcomes and keep people safer. And yet in both instances, the minute that extra knowledge becomes known, it becomes suffocating and horrifying, robbing people of their free

6. Spielberg, *Minority Report.*

will. Indeed, it was not only the talmudic rabbis who were wary of heavenly voices telling society what to do. Even pop culture today, albeit couched in different terms, shares that same apprehension.

Therefore, the TBD must remain unknown, and we must continue to strive together for the best decisions we can, each with our own separate views and opinions. Without all the positions coming into contact, mixing with each other in honest debate, thereby producing a single Actual Path which we hope and admit will on average be closer to the TBD than if just one of us had used our own opinion all the time, the entire exercise of life would be pointless. It would collapse into simple authoritarianism directed either by God or by the most powerful human at any given time and place (or by the inescapable Orwellian information in the two films referenced above). By the same token, however, each individual must strive to make their opinion known, heard, and understood. Further, each individual must actually believe that their opinion is indeed the best one, the closest to the TBD, and yet at the same time know that the TBD is ultimately unknowable and that it logically may end up being closer to someone else's opinion rather than to their own. This knowledge makes it easier when the time for action has come—once the deliberations are over, the votes cast, and the ballots counted—for each individual to capitulate to the Actual Path rather than continue ad infinitum to press for their own individual opinion.

REPUBLICANS AND DEMOCRATS

Let's switch back to modern politics. Imagine there is an election approaching. What would happen if just before voting each person had to actually say out loud, "I, so-and-so, do hereby declare that although I am voting for candidate X, I understand that this in no way changes the fact that the better candidate may actually be Y." In other words, everyone would have to explicitly acknowledge that though for example you might think that path A is the correct way to proceed, that the TBD might actually be closer to path B. It is not so easy to believe both at the same time: that you, after carefully thinking it over, think that A is best, and yet at the same time understand that the TBD might in fact be B. Why is this? As above, the data which is available to you is not the sum total of all the data, and the way in which you analyze the data is not the only way it could be analyzed, your biases are not the only possible biases that one could have, etc.; so the ultimate TBD might not always line up exactly with what you perceive to be the best decision in every instance. In fact, one might go so far as to say that it would be very strange or coincidental or weird if in fact the two did line up completely. So for example, if there are ten issues that make up the current political agenda (I actually counted approximately sixty issues on the 2020 Democratic Party Platform[7] and approximately ninety issues on the 2016 Republican Party Platform[8], which was readopted without changes for 2020) and you think about each one and come to your own conclusion on each one, then it would be very odd, even unreasonable, to expect that your chosen position would agree with the TBD all the way down the line on each of the ten issues (or on each of the sixty Democratic issues or on each of the ninety Republican issues). It would be much more likely that you would be correct on some issues but not on others. That would just statistically make the most sense.

Now I suppose you might argue that if your position on the ten issues all stems from one certain world view (like Democrat or Republican), then if you have the correct world view you'll get to the TBD on each of the ten issues (or on the entire party platform). But that may be oversimplifying things a bit. For one thing, much of politics is simply local and not beholden to a certain worldview, and second, many political issues are not actually the result of the logical extension of basic principles but rather an amalgamation of the opinions of various special interest groups such that there is often not a unifying logic to the various talking points held by political parties. In addition, who's to say your so-called "worldview" is correct at all? If it happens not to be, then according to your own logic (that your correct worldview is leading you to be

7. "Party Platform: The Democratic Platform."
8. "Republican Platform 2016."

correct on all the issues at hand) you'd be dead wrong on every single issue—all sixty of them or all ninety of them. Maybe you're okay with a fifty-fifty chance of being right (since there are only two political parties)—in Las Vegas those would be pretty good odds. But are those really the only two worldviews? What about the Green party? The Libertarian party? The Socialist party? Now your odds of not being wrong on every single issue are down to only one in five. The point is that everyone should try to make the best decision they can while at the same time realizing that their decision may or may not be the same as the TBD.

This type of thinking—knowing that despite you're trying as best you can to figure things out, think things through, and come up with your honest, best position on each issue, you still might not actually get to the TBD—is difficult. In fact, it is not only counterintuitive, but it can potentially be totally paralyzing. Because if you can't even trust your own internal decision-making then what's the point? Why even try at all? Why go through all the mental effort if you're just going to be wrong most of the time? It might seem that you could save yourself a lot of trouble just by flipping a coin.

But the point is that in order for the system to work, we each must think it through for ourselves, come to our own decisions, hash them out with others in public debate, and then collectively decide the course of action to take, from which the Actual Path emerges. In every instance this collective result, the Actual Path, will agree with some people's position and disagree with others. But even though we all know that our individual positions may be wrong some of the time, we also know that without going through the exercise together no decisions can ever be made. It also means, and this is key, that when the Actual Path disagrees with our individual choice we can accept that dissonance; that we don't have to be so incensed by the disparity that we call the other side murderers and work tirelessly day and night to undo the decision that has been made in every instance of disagreement.

MODERN POLITICAL DECISION-MAKING THEORY? OR ANCIENT WISDOM?

This theory of shared decision-making which speaks of two opposing opinions, the Actual Path and the Theoretically Better Decision (TBD), is modern, philosophical, and perhaps a bit academic in nature; but it can also be found within the ancient text of the Bible, the guiding wisdom of the ancient Israelites, Judaism, and the modern State of Israel. Why does that matter? The relationship between the United States and Israel is often conceptualized as America the 250-year-old superpower being a sort of big brother to the little and sprightly seventy-five-year-old Israel. America, as the older and wiser sibling, is therefore able to teach Israel how to better function in the modern world of grown-up nations. Often we see American diplomats preaching how they know what is best for Israel. They seem to view Israel as if it were a cute little child who thinks it knows what it wants even though the parent knows better. They sometimes speak as if they realize that though little Israel might think it wants one thing, the older and wiser American parent knows that a different path may actually be necessary. The poor young Israel may just need the more mature America to gently shepherd it in the correct direction, like a parent coaxing its child to make better decisions. However, if one considers the modern State of Israel to be the inheritor of the traditions of Judaism, which itself was the inheritor of the two ancient Israelite kingdoms and the ancient wisdom of the biblical nation of Israel, then perhaps the roles should be reversed. In this case, it would be the much older and wiser Israel who might be able to teach something to the relatively younger America. Because the wisdom of ancient Israel empirically has allowed it to survive for so long, much longer in fact that the United States has been in existence, it would be well worth it for America to take note of the wisdom which has sustained Israel and Judaism through the ages. The fact that this decision-making theory may be found within the Bible itself lends credence to it as a successful time-tested theory, more than simply the opinion of one modern individual.

THE ARK OF THE COVENANT

Where can this theory be found within the Bible? Let us turn to the biblical description of one of the most well-known ancient artifacts the world has ever known: the ark of the covenant. You probably have seen the movie *Indiana Jones and the Raiders Of the Lost Ark.*[9] The movie portrays Indiana Jones, an archeologist played by Harrison Ford, finding the lost holy ark of the covenant. In the final scene the ark is finally found and opened. Those assembled slowly remove the cover and peer inside. I won't spoil the movie for anyone who hasn't seen it, but that scene is consistent with most modern thoughts about the so-called power of the ark. Most people would agree that the importance of the ark and the source of its holy, supernatural powers lay in its contents; among other things, the stone tablets of the Ten Commandments, carved by the very "finger of God."[10] The holy ark was to be feared and revered for what it contained. The power of God lay inside, under the covering, which was carefully removed in that final scene in the movie.

However, this is actually not the case at all. The plain text of the Bible makes quite clear that when Moses would enter the sanctuary, God would speak to him not from the ark itself as one might think, but rather from outside the ark. In fact, God's voice would emanate precisely from the empty space just above the top of the ark. You may be familiar with pictures of the ark. Its cover was made of pure gold. There were two golden cherubs, child-like angels, positioned at opposite ends facing each other. Their wings were stretched inwards and upwards toward each other, forming a covering over the ark. It was from within this empty space—above the ark, between the two cherubs facing one to another, and under their spread wings—that the voice of God would emanate as it spoke to Moses. Let us examine the biblical text to see how our theory of shared decision-making is hidden inside.

9. Spielberg. *Raiders of the Lost Ark.*

10. Exod 31:18 and Deut 9:10, translation adapted from *Koren Tanakh, Magerman Edition.*

If we open the Bible to Exod 25:18–22, where the cherubs of the ark are first described, we read the following:

ועשית שנים כרבים זהב מקשה תעשה אתם משני קצות הכפרת:
ועשה כרוב אחד מקצה מזה וכרוב אחד מקצה מן הכפרת
תעשו את הכרבים על שני קצותיו: והיו הכרבים פרשי כנפים
למעלה סככים בכנפיהם על הכפרת ופניהם איש אל אחיו אל
הכפרת יהיו פני הכרבים: ונתת את הכפרת על הארן מלמעלה
ואל הארן תתן את העדת אשר אתן אליך: ונועדתי לך שם
ודברתי אתך מעל הכפרת מבין שני הכרבים אשר על ארן העדת
את כל אשר אצוה אותך אל בני ישראל:

Ve'asita shenayim keruvim zahav mikshah ta'aseh otam mishenei ketzot hakkapporet. Va'aseh keruv echad mik-katzah mizzeh ucheruv-echad mikkatzah mizzeh min-hakkapporet ta'asu et-hakkeruvim al-shenei ketzotav. Vehayu hakkeruvim poresei chenafayim lema'lah so-chechim bechanfeihem al hakkapporet ufeneihem ish el-achiv el-hakkapporet yihyu penei hakkeruvim. Venatatta et-hakkapporet al-ha'aron milma'elah ve'el-ha'aron titten et-ha'edut asher etten eleicha. Veno'adti lecha sham vedib-barti ittecha me'al hakkapporet mibbein shenei hakkeru-vim asher al-aron ha'edut et kol-asher atzavveh otecha el-benei yisra'el.

And thou shalt make two cherubs of gold, of beaten work shalt thou make them, at the two ends of the covering. And make one cherub on the one end, and the other cherub on the other end: of the covering shall you make the cherubs on the two ends of it. And the cherubs shall stretch out their wings on high, overspreading the covering with their wings, and their faces shall look one to another; toward the covering shall the faces of the cherubs be. And thou shalt put the covering above, upon the ark; and in the ark thou shalt put the Testimony that I shall give thee. And there I will meet with thee, and I will speak with thee from above the covering, from between the two cherubs which are upon the ark of the Testimony, of all things which I will give thee in commandment to the children of Israel.[11]

The text doesn't simply say, "Make two cherubs and place them at opposite sides on top of the ark." Curiously, in those two verses the word "end" or "edge" is repeated four different times (underlined in the text above). It is axiomatic in Jewish biblical exegesis that there are no extra words in the Bible, so that the obvious and otherwise unnecessary repetition of this word must be telling us something. The interesting thing is that the modern Hebrew word for "extremist" is קיצוני—*kitzoni* (from the same root קצה—*katzeh*), since an extremist is one who stands at the end or edge of societal norms, opinions, etc. If we understand the word "edge" instead as "extremist," we would understand the two cherubs to be representing two extremes of opinion. They are each placed at opposite "edges" of the ark, as if to say that they reside at the extreme opposite "ends" of sociopolitical discourse.

The next verse talks about their wings and says they should be extended upwards, each facing toward the other, and that their spread wings should be covering the top of the ark. The sentence is underlined in the text above. The word פרשי—*poresei* (from the root פרש—*paras*) is used here to mean "spread," as in "they should spread their wings upward," but if the letter ש—*shin* is rendered slightly differently, as an "sh" instead of an "s" (which in Hebrew is the exact same letter with only a different pronunciation), then the word can also mean an understanding or an explanation. (For example, a "פירוש רשי—*perush rashi*" is an explanation by Rashi, the famous thirteenth century Jewish commentator, and the "מפורשים—*m'forshim*" are the Sages, the explainers of the Torah, all from the same root—פרש—*parash*.) Read in this way, the verse would be saying that the understanding or explanation of the wings should be oriented upwards. The upward orientation indicates a heavenward orientation, a universal metaphor for honesty or truth. This means that each "extremist" cherub should have their "explanations," their arguments, oriented upwards towards

---

11. Translation adapted from *Koren Tanakh, Magerman Edition*.

truth. That is, they should be debating with honest intent, solely to arrive at the real truth of the matter, rather than for petty personal gain, power, or money.

The next word of interest in the same underlined verse is סככים—*sochechim*. This is rendered as "overspreading" in the English translation, but more basically is the plural verb form of "to cover," so that a more basic translation would read "shall stretch out their wings on high, covering the ark cover with their wings." This word in Hebrew for covering has a somewhat unique meaning. It shares a root with the Hebrew word סכך—*s'chach*, which is used on the Jewish holiday of Sukkot, the festival of booths, to cover the sukkah booth. The covering of the sukkah has very specific characteristics and it entirely defines the space underneath it, so much so that the legality of the entire structure hinges almost entirely on the nature of that special covering, the סכך—*s'chach*. In other words, the function of that unique word for covering is not simply to connote keeping out the elements or hiding something or protecting some pre-existing object, as would be the typical connotation of the word "to cover." Rather, this specific word is used to define a space which was not defined before; specifically in the case of Sukkot, the space underneath the sukkah covering, thereby defining it as a sacred space.

So too here, the two pairs of wings reaching upwards define the space underneath them. Metaphorically, the two extremist cherubs, with their wings/arguments being oriented upwards toward truth, define a particular space. That space is bounded by the extremists themselves on either side and by the arguments/ explanations/opinions which each one shares. It is precisely this space from which God speaks. In the language of our previous theory of decision-making, each cherub represents one of the two competing opinions, say husband and wife, or Republican and Democrat. The TBD is clearly God's word. The Actual Path taken, being a wandering amalgam of the differing extremist opinions may be represented in this stylized representation as the midpoint between the two cherubs. The interesting thing to note is that in this perfect scenario (quite literally carved in gold as per God's instructions), when the arguments are oriented heavenwards towards honesty and truth, then God's word emanates from that exact space between the two cherubs. The TBD and the Actual Path then coincide. When everything is done with true and honest intent, the Actual Path approaches and indeed becomes coincident with God's word, the TBD.

Note that God's voice didn't have to come from that empty space. It was not logically the most obvious place. It didn't even need to be mentioned at all, for that matter. Why is it even relevant what exact spot God's voice comes from? It would surely have been enough to have simply said that Moses went into the Tent of Meeting and would speak with God, or would hear God's voice. Why specify a certain locus at all? Further, if there are two faces right there (the cherubs), why not have the voice come from them? Or if not from them, why not from the ark itself? The fact that God's voice specifically comes from the seemingly empty space defined by the upwards oriented wings (arguments) of the two opposing cherubs (extremists) makes the metaphor all the more compelling. In summary, the physical layout of the top of the ark of the covenant is metaphorically telling us that when two opposing sides in an argument are debating in good faith, that the resulting agreement reached will be as close as possible to God's word, as it were. It is also telling us that the best way to get as close as possible to God's word, to ultimate truth, to the TBD, is exactly through the process of debating one's adversary honestly and truthfully. Finally, it is telling us that this approach of mutual debate will always more accurately reflect the TBD than if either side were able to force their will to be done unilaterally.

Please do not make the mistake of taking this schema too literally and therefore oversimplifying reality. The ark cover is a physical representation which can help us to remember these important aspects of shared decision-making. It does not mean that the Actual Path or the Theoretically Better Decision (TBD) are always going to be a simple average at the exact midpoint between the two extremes. It does not mean that we can look at our viewpoint, look at our adversary's viewpoint, and then predict in advance that the "God's-eye view" is in every case going to be the precise arithmetic mean. Importantly, this does not mean that we somehow have to compromise our own ideals by watering them down to bring them closer to those of our political opponents. Remember, the process of finding the Actual Path is difficult and will be different in every case. Sometimes one side will be convinced by the other, sometimes one side will garner enough support to force its will democratically to be done, sometimes external factors will influence the decision to go one way or the other and sometimes compromises will be made taking into account past or future decisions by the same parties. The theory we are developing does not alter the real-time negotiation of getting to an Actual Path, nor does it prejudge the ultimate location of that Actual Path. It does, however, remind us that there is a difference between debating to win and debating to find the truth. Recall that the wings/arguments of the cherubs are not pointed directly at each other, as they would be if the intent was simply to defeat one's opponent. They are pointed upwards toward truth. This is perhaps a subtle distinction, but it alters the way we conceive of winning. In the schema of the ark cover, winning means finding an Actual Path which is as close to the TBD as possible. In the ideal scenario then, both sides are winners. This stands in stark contrast to the situation where each side is debating to win, where by definition there can be only one winner and one loser.

DRINKING YOUR OWN KOOL-AID

But what about gaming the system? We touched on this briefly in the preceding discussion about shared decision-making between husband and wife, where we noted that if the husband wanted to pull the average over time closer to his position, he could game the system by artificially making his opinion more extreme as a simple bargaining tactic. The analogous situation regarding the ark of the covenant would be if one side, one cherub as it were, was so convinced that they were correct that they wanted to force the "middle" space (Actual Path) closer to their position. In the schema of the ark, the stubborn cherub would move itself farther away to the side. Thus the "middle" space between the two would end up moving over toward the wayward cherub. While this may seem a bit awkward when considering the cherubs on the ark cover, this is unfortunately a very common phenomenon in real life.

Many involved in political debate today are prone to the societally destructive habit of artificially inflating the extremeness of their views as a simple negotiating tactic. In other words, in their quest for victory they feel it necessary to start with maximalist demands. That's what every good negotiator does, after all. The assumption is that they can bargain down from there, so they will end up "compromising" at a point which they still find acceptable. This is obvious to anyone who has ever been shopping in an old-style, middle-eastern market. If you're willing to pay ten dollars for an item, you never actually offer ten dollars up front. Rather, you start by offering five dollars, then you work your way up through a series of offers and counteroffers, until you end up compromising at ten dollars, the amount you had originally wanted to spend in the first place.

In politics this means that people sometimes make up a fake starting point. They know it's not really true, but it's a great bargaining tactic. If you start way back there, you'll probably end up getting a great deal. This is a problem for two reasons. First, it is simply dishonest and therefore if the person or politician ends up "winning" then the resulting Actual Path will move (falsely) over time closer to the position of one side relative to the other. This will undoubtedly be worse for the country because it will most likely end up moving the Actual Path farther away from the TBD, similar to what would happen in a case of pure coercion where the Actual Path would be moved purposefully toward one side in all cases. But even worse, those tasked with making the tactically more extreme arguments often end up convincing themselves of their own lies. When this happens to both sides, the two sides end up eventually believing their own more extreme positions, and thus continually move farther and farther apart. Have both sides in the US simply begun to drink too much of their own political

Kool-Aid? So much so that the goalposts keep moving farther and farther away from each other? Each side seems to wonder, "How could the other side actually believe all that stuff? Or do they just say that so they'll get a better deal?" Perhaps in the beginning that was true—perhaps it still is with respect to the latest iteration. It may seem like a cliché but when you say it enough times, eventually you start believing it yourself.

Getting back to the description of the ark cover, does the biblical text have anything to say about this? In fact it does. The text makes a point of saying that the covering of the ark was to be made of pure gold, and that the two cherubs (the two extremists, in our allegorical interpretation) were to be made from the covering itself, in one piece. In other words, the cherubs are not separate pieces which were simply placed on top of the ark. They were therefore not mobile. They were not even constructed individually and then bolted or soldered onto the covering. Rather they were integral to the cover itself, made from the same single piece of gold, fixed in place permanently, each at the edge of the space defined by the dimensions of the ark cover. This tells us metaphorically that part of what honest "upward oriented" debate entails is the honest representation of one's opinion, not the arbitrary movement of one's opinion to a more extreme position just to game the system.

Why would someone engage in the obviously destructive behavior of falsely representing their own beliefs as more extreme than they really are? As discussed above, it depends on your orientation; on how you frame the negotiation. Are you negotiating to win? If so, undoubtedly the most commonly held view of why we have political negotiations, then this negotiating strategy makes perfect sense. But what if we were to reorient ourselves such that we are debating to find the truth, to find the TBD rather than to simply win at all costs? With this new orientation, an admittedly less common one, it becomes clear that this strategy will never work.

ATONEMENT

But how serious is this schema, really? Everyone knows that politicians are not always completely honest. What would happen if people started arguing falsely as described above, or started thinking that only they knew what was right, or thinking there was no need to debate the other side anymore, or even no need to acknowledge the other side at all? Does the biblical text anticipate any of these common human failings? To answer this we must note what the ark covering with the two cherubs is called. The name given to the ark cover is the כפרת—*kaporet*. This word comes from the same root as the word for atonement. It comes from the same root as יום כפור—*Yom Kippur*, the Jewish holiday called the Day of Atonement. Perhaps this is telling us that when these human failings of dishonest, self-serving, polarization accumulate, one way we atone and fix ourselves is by looking to this model of honest, true, respectful, and upwards oriented debate which will then lead to God's voice becoming manifest, as it were, and the TBD once again becoming apparent.

In fact, during the Yom Kippur service in the time of the ancient Jewish temple, when the high priest would go into the holy of holies where the ark was located (which was only done on this one particular day of the year), one of main sacrificial rites he would perform was to take the blood of the sacrifices for that day and sprinkle it toward the ark covering (the כפרת—*kaporet*—atonement) bearing the two cherubs. Observant Jews today still read the reenactment of this rite every year on Yom Kippur. During this ritual the holy of holies was full of smoke from the incense offering so it is unlikely that even the high priest saw the scene in the room with any clarity. But we can imagine what it would have looked like, after the several sprinklings of blood from the sacrifices of that solemn day. It would have looked as if each golden cherub, each "extremist," was bleeding.

Perhaps we should dwell on that image for a moment. It would have appeared, metaphorically, as if the two sides of society had mortally wounded each other with the dishonesty and savagery of their false opinions. Does that sound familiar? Does that not describe the situation in America today? Two bleeding extremist camps facing off against each other, rather than manifesting the truthful, honest roles for which they were designed? Part of what the ancient Israelites atoned for each Yom Kippur was the failure to heed these lessons. It would behoove us in America to not repeat the same mistakes, lest we remain locked in bloody dishonest combat which may yet rip the country apart.

THIS IS NOT ABOUT THE CENTER

This is not just another plea for centrism. If you are a right-wing Republican or a left-wing Democrat, this is not about forcing you to move to some average, diluted middle ground. Again, the bleeding cherubs on the ark cover are to be seen only as a stylized representation. They do not imply that today's radical right and progressive left are each exactly equidistant from some morally correct center. On the contrary, those on the right and those on the left must continue to vigorously voice their opinions. But they must do so honestly. They must remember that they are ultimately each striving not to win, but to reach a TBD. Finally, they must realize that wherever the Actual Path ends up, toward the center or otherwise, we must all traverse it together.

Do not be misled by the religious imagery here. If this imagery speaks to you, wonderful. If not, remember that this is simply the language of the Bible, the language used to communicate the ancient wisdom of the Israelites. Do not forget that the wisdom itself has sustained the Israelites, the Jewish people, and the State of Israel for three thousand years. In this sense it is as empirical and scientific as any political theory could be. The cherubs on the ark are each of us. Each of us individually has a role to play. There is no simple, systemic structural change we can make which will automatically make everything right without individual people struggling on their own to act differently. We all must internalize the lessons in order to change the culture and therefore society as a whole. If we each take heed of the necessity that each of us must argue our opinions to the best of our abilities with an honest intent to reach the TBD, and we all individually recognize that the TBD is ultimately unknowable, then we can satisfy ourselves with the faith that the Actual Path upon which we find ourselves will be coincident with that TBD. But if we try to hijack the system so that not all the views are heard, or so that one set of views simply overpowers the others, or that the end result is shifted toward our preferred side through dishonest and false representation of our actual opinions, then although we may indeed end up closer to our personal preferred opinion, we can rest assured that this will be farther away from the TBD. This will produce at a minimum a worse outcome for the country, if not the exact hateful and perpetual conflict we see today.

Chapter Two

Debate among Tribes

CHAPTER 1 DISCUSSED SHARED decision-making between individuals and touched on the appropriate role of societal extremes as represented by the cherubs on the ark cover. We will begin chapter 2 with a discussion of debate and disagreement among different groups in society by looking at the Talmud, the Jewish compendium of legal debates. In the several hundred years after the destruction of the second Jewish commonwealth by the Roman Empire in the year 70 of the Common Era, the Talmud documented myriad arguments about the details of Jewish law and about the basic practices which defined what it meant to be part of the nation. For the purposes of this discussion the details are not important. The methodology is, however, of paramount importance. In every argument, all opinions are recorded and respected.

In the previous Talmudic story about the oven of Achnai, the minority opinion was felt to be so far outside the norm, and the actions of the opinion holder so egregious, that the rabbi was excommunicated from the community. In that time there was no punishment more severe than that. There was no indictor of the depth of disagreement stronger than that. Yet, his opinion, indeed the entire story even to the point of recording that God God's self agreed with him, was preserved and respected. Did the compilers of the Talmud worry that one day some new radical hot-head might come upon this story, read how God agreed with the dissenting opinion, and dedicate himself to resurrecting what he believed to be the correct opinion in that case, and perhaps other "wrong" opinions as well? Surely that point must have been considered. Did they consider instead of recording that opinion, cancelling it, not allowing it to be spoken, censoring it? Surely they considered that. But in the end, the inclusivity of maintaining the opinion as part of the national discourse won out.

Certainly we have to struggle with the limits of free speech. But in an honest competition for ideas in our national story we can learn the lesson from the Talmud that respecting all opinions helps us grow and helps the story speak to all people. The Talmud knew that arguing and disagreement in and of itself was not an unhealthy sign of fracturing but rather a healthy sign of intellectual prowess as community members struggle to better understand the best way forward.

The preservation of such minority opinions went further than the simple recording of their existence. Often a full explanation of the details of the logic employed, the values upheld, and the justification for their opinions was recorded as well. This was important because a point of logic, line of reasoning, or value upheld in a minority opinion could often be resurrected at some later point to serve as the basis for an entirely new position on an unrelated topic. This is a far different mindset than the current one in our country today which too often tries to shut down dissenting opinions, censor articles, ban content, or heckle opposing speakers off stage.

The talmudic sages also knew that debate could not last forever; that eventually the practicalities of life demand concrete decisions and actions. This means inevitably that there will be winners and losers; people who end up agreeing with the final decision and those who disagree. But by emphasizing the debate itself as much as the outcome, the sages of the Talmud were able to accomplish two things simultaneously. First, they were able to de-emphasize the simple actions that society does by placing equal weight on the decision-making process and by respecting all decisions, even if only one decision is ultimately the way things are done. Second, they were able to ensure that the decision finally undertaken was the best one possible, the closest to the TBD on average, because they, and indeed all of society, knew that all honest and true opinions had been taken into account.

We must keep in mind that it was assumed that these arguing rabbis were in pursuit only of the truth as best they could perceive it, rather than power or personal gain. It should also be noted that the reason for this assumption is not simply because they were great and learned rabbis. Indeed they were great and learned, but an important additional factor was that none of them were "professional rabbis." In other words, none of the talmudic rabbis earned their living from being a rabbi. They all had other jobs. What is the relevance of this seemingly trivial fact? It served to disconnect their ability to earn a living from their talmudic debates. Their livelihood was therefore not dependent on how many talmudic arguments they "won." This is in sharp contrast to today's political class, most of whom are professional politicians, professional pollsters, professional political staffers, professional policy analysts, etc. This professional political class not only sees their personal financial success directly related to the quality and number of political wins they accumulate, but indeed often their entire self-identity and sense of self-worth is wrapped up in winning and the attendant financial and social success it brings.

This talmudic method of argumentation which respects all opinions appears to operate on an individual level. That is, it speaks about individual people debating with each other. What about group dynamics in society at large? What about groups arguing with each other, as we see today? Is there some ancient wisdom which has guided the successful Israelites, Judaism, and Israel regarding the social dynamics of conflicting sociopolitical groups?

THE VESTMENTS OF THE HIGH PRIEST

Let us look once again to the text of the Bible itself. Exodus 28 contains a description of the vestments of the high priest. There are eight different garments and the description is quite compli-cated. Clearly there is a lot of symbolism related to the different garments because each is described in exquisite detail. But there is one thing which stands out. As we have seen, it is axiomatic in biblical literature that when a word is repeated it is meant to emphasize something important. Here, it is not just a word which is repeated but an entire physical motif. The high priest quite liter-ally wears on his person the names of each of the twelve tribes of Israel—not once, but twice. The first iteration of this relates to the ephod, a kind of apron held up by two shoulder straps. On the shoulder clasp of each shoulder strap were two stones in golden settings, one on each shoulder. Engraved on each stone were the names of the twelve sons of Israel, six on each stone, from which the twelve tribes of Israel were born. But as if this wasn't enough to make the point, the high priest also wore a breastplate with twelve individual stones set on it. Each stone had engraved on it one of the names of the tribes of Israel.

What does all of this mean? What is the symbolism? I be-lieve this symbolizes two important things. First, we might think that the ultimate symbolism which the one high priest is meant to embody would be unity. We might expect that the ultimate goal is that the children of Israel should be unified in their common mission and identity and that the symbolism therefore should be reflective of this. After all, Judaism is quite specific about the unity and oneness of God, so it would stand to reason that the Israelites themselves should strive to emulate that unity. One might then ex-pect the symbology of the office of the high priest to reflect this by using a shared symbol which all the tribes had in common, such as perhaps the menorah (the seven branched candelabra used in the tabernacle and later in the temple). Therefore it is a bit jarring to see the symbolism on the high priest reflecting not oneness, not unity, but rather the fractured complexity of the twelve separate tribes of Israel. It is even more jarring to see this symbolism not once, but twice.

In fact, the high priest did wear a symbol of divine oneness on his forehead: the golden head plate which bore the words "קדש

ליקוק—*kodesh l'adonai*—Holy to God."[1] Even so, this was a single symbol, whereas the symbol of the twelve tribes was repeated twice. This, I believe, comes to teach us that complexity is meant to be a defining characteristic of the nation, so long as that complexity is oriented toward a common identity and a shared story. In the biblical construct we are not all meant to agree with each other, nor are we meant to be convinced by a single tribe which is the smartest or the most correct. Rather, we are meant to have a multiplicity of opinions, of tribes, which when aggregated together give rise to a successful whole.

The fact that we today might have different tribes—Democrat and Republican, left and right, pro-Trump and never-Trump, moderate Democrat and progressive Liberal, black and white, Hispanic, Asian, Native American, etc.—is immaterial. The tribes can change. But the theory still holds, even regarding the new or changed tribes. Each tribe remains important in its own right, meant to be in perpetual discussion with all the others. They are not meant to be swallowed up by either the strongest in a show of force, nor by the most victimized in a show of moral purity, leaving only one. We are meant to have an enduring social community of different tribes, all in dialogue with each other, which can change through time. In a sense, the symbolism of the twelve tribes repeated twice on the garments of the biblical high priest parallels the fifty individual stars on the American flag. Although the bald eagle is a unified symbol of the entire country, our most important national icon, the American flag, does not feature a single icon or picture, but rather a depiction of the many different tribes/states which make up our union.

THIS IS NOT PLURALISM

This picture of multiple tribes maintaining their own separate identities yet contributing to a unified whole is not simply another form of pluralism. Pluralism has many definitions. Politically it

---

1. Exod 28:36, translation is my own.

can refer to a system with multiple centers of power or to the acceptance within a political system of differing viewpoints. In the United States this is a given. We have three separate centers of power ensconced in our three independent branches of government, and different political viewpoints are built into the system through political parties. In the United States when people talk about pluralism as a philosophical outlook which can help mollify our divisiveness, they often mean something akin to religious pluralism, which is the acceptance of different religious doctrines as equally valid. In simple terms, it is the belief that it is okay if we disagree because we can all be right.

Pluralism in this sense is often used to diffuse disagreement by simply trying to brush it aside (without actually resolving anything). It does not require that either side acquiesce to the other's demands or beliefs because both sides can be equally correct at the same time. The problem with this type of pluralism is that it too often requires the parties to suspend logic and reason. There are often positions or beliefs which at least on the surface are mutually exclusive—if one is true, the other cannot also be true. It is simply dishonest to proffer in the name of pluralism, no matter how fashionable it may be, that your adversary is as correct as you are, especially when you feel in your heart that they are not. The difference between pluralism and the solutions offered in this book is that the theories in this book do not require either side to suspend their belief that they are correct and their adversary is incorrect. Rather, all sides continue to believe in their unique rightness while at the same time conceding that all sides are honestly doing their best to seek the best position possible in a world of imperfect information. Each side sees the problem from a different perspective and therefore attempts to solve the problem with different sets of information leading to different proposed solutions. Further, each side understands that the interplay of the different proposed solutions by each party, all of whom believe themselves to be correct given the information to which they have access, is what will ultimately give rise to the best solution. Although practically the results may be similar, this is quite different than simply throwing our hands up and saying, "Lets stop fighting—we can all be right!"

WHERE IS THE UNITY?

Acknowledging our different tribes and our disagreements is important, but where then, is the true unity that seems so foundational to any nation? In the biblical tradition, that is left to God. Only God is one; we are not. For a religious person this may make perfect sense on its own. What does this mean to a secular American today? It means that ultimate oneness is left to be aspirational. Or perhaps, it means that the ultimate oneness we seek in America today resides in the national structure of our common union. It is where we point ourselves, what we are aiming for although we may never actually reach it. We must remain separate tribes, with separate opinions, always arguing with each other, always respectful of each other, always knowing that the unity we seek is ultimately unknowable, as is the TBD in the theory discussed earlier. Only in our remaining as distinct tribes can we hope to eventually reach, in a common paradox, the national unity to which we strive. In the language of the Israelites, true unity is left to God, not humanity. In our modern language, true unity is aspirational. We are meant to have respectful disagreement and debate across all our different tribes.

This may sound easy or obvious but it is not. Most Democrats today feel that their view is correct and that if only they could somehow force the Republicans to see the light and become Democrats, then the country could be governed as they know it should be. Most Republicans feel the same way in reverse. But that would be a false unity. That kind of unity, the kind imposed by one group on all the others, cannot work. Politically we know this to be true because that is what occurred in the single party Soviet Union and in single party Communist China. It is perhaps worth dwelling on this point a bit longer. Most right-wing Republicans today (or progressive Democrats) know that we are not supposed to be a single party system and know that we are supposed to have debate and discussion between all parties, etc. At the same time, most of them believe that their vision truly is correct. According to our previous discussion of shared decision-making, that is as it should be. However, how many right-wing Republicans (or progressive Democrats) are able to take the next step? How many are able to realize that the Theoretically Better Decision for the country is not—cannot be by definition—their own exact vision (despite their vigorous belief that it should be so), but rather must be, by definition, a complex amalgam resulting from the interplay between them and their adversaries across the aisle which cannot be known or even predicted in advance? I am not aware of any data on this question, but it seems to me that the current answer would be very few.

THE SHEMA

The above discussion about the vestments of the high priest is somewhat esoteric, as there is no Jewish temple today and there is no functioning office of the high priest. However, this theory may be found in another biblical text which remains in common use even today. I am referring to one of the shortest and most well known prayers in Judaism, one which is repeated at least twice daily by observant Jews to this day. It is commonly called the Shema, it is only six words long, and it is a direct quote from a passage in the Bible. The prayer reads as follows: שמע ישראל יקוק אלקנו יקוק אחד—"*Shema yisraʼel adonai eloheinu adonai echad.*"[2] It is most commonly translated as, "Hear O Israel: the Lord our God, the Lord is One." This prayer has a multitude of interpretations, encompassing different layers of meaning, from the simple surface meaning, to allegorical story, to mystical-kabbalistic interpretation. Our purpose here is not to undertake a deep dive into the wide array of literature and thought about this prayer, but rather simply to offer one insight into how it may be understood in a way which dovetails with our previous discussion about the

---

2. Deut 6:4, translation is my own.

aspirational oneness of God (or the aspirational oneness of our United States) versus the fractured and tribal existence of our individual lives.

Grammatically, the prayer may be broken down into three two-word phrases: "שמע ישראל—*Shema yisra'el*—Hear O Israel"; "יקוק אלקנו—*adonai eloheinu*—the Lord our God"; "יקוק אחד—*adonai echad*—the Lord is One*." The first phrase is usually understood as a kind of introduction, whereas the last two phrases are taken to be the actual information being communicated. In this vein, it is usually understood as something akin to "listen up! The Lord is our God! The Lord is One!" But what if the first phrase is more than just "listen up"? There are many interpretations which focus on the exact meaning of that first word, "שמע—*shema*—hear." It commonly means to listen or to hear. Some interpretations focus on the active aspect of the word, instructing us to listen actively rather than passively hearing. Others focus on the connotation of this specific word for hearing which includes an element of understanding and therefore connotes more than the simple biological function of hearing sounds with our ears. But in all of these cases, whatever kind of hearing one is talking about, it is generally agreed that the object of the hearing/understanding is the content of the next two phrases, namely that we are supposed to hear/listen/understand that the Lord is our God and that the Lord is One.

But what if the listening is a command in and of itself? What if each phrase is a totally separate command each of which stands entirely on its own? If we read it this way, the first phrase of the text would not be saying, "Listen up, I've got something to tell you," but rather, simply "Listen, Israel—period." Or "Keep listening, Israel." What does this mean? In the context of our previous discussions about unity, different tribes, talmudic debate, and shared decision-making, this would mean that one must always keep listening to the other side, to other tribes, and to other minority points of view.

The next phrase, "יקוק אלקנו—*adonai eloheinu*—the Lord is our God," would then be seen as a reminder of our aspiration to reach the TBD, because God in this schema represents the ultimate and correct Theoretically Better Decision—the heavenly voice in the talmudic story of the oven of Achnai or the "God's-eye view" in our original discussion of shared decision-making. This second phrase is then the metaphorical flag planted in the ground which marks the goalpost. It states quite simply the object of our common striving.

The third phrase, "יקוק אחד—*adonai echad*—the Lord is One," is as much a reminder of what is One as to what is not. We individually in our personal lives and in our collective political lives as well often seek to determine what is best and then attempt to persuade or coerce the world around us to uniformly fit that image of reality which we ourselves have created. This third phrase reminds us that true unity is aspirational. It is left to the realm of the divine. We are not One, nor should we delude ourselves into thinking that it is our place to become One or to make our world One. It is only in the listening to the multiplicity of voices and opinions which are oriented towards truth (God, in this prayer), that we can somehow end up asymptotically approaching (though never actually reaching) that ultimate and infinite Oneness which in this schema is reserved for the divine. In the language of our theory of shared decision-making, only the TBD (the God's-eye view) is one; our individual or collective opinions are not, nor should they be.

To put this once again in a modern, American context, the wisdom of this prayer is telling us first, ("שמע ישראל—*Shema yisra'el*—Hear O Israel") to always keep listening. When we impose our will on others, we are not listening. When we quash debate or cancel speakers with whom we disagree, we are not listening. When we label the other side untouchable, we are not listening. Second, ("יקוק אלקנו—*adonai eloheinu*—the Lord is our God") the object of our striving is the common American good to which we all aspire—perhaps that we all have a shot at the American dream and that America be a force for good throughout the world; and the TBDs which will take us there. Third, ("יקוק אחד—*adonai echad*—the Lord is One") the common American good is a singular goal to which we all aspire. However, neither the means by which we get there, nor the debates we have in pursuit of that common goal are singular, nor should they be, lest we veer off into the realm of authoritarianism.

Again, this is not easy. Normally, if one is trying to get somewhere one pushes in that specific direction. But in this case, each of us must push in a different direction from where we actually want to go. How so? Because each of us knows that we want to arrive at the TBD and each of us knows that this will almost never line up exactly with our personal opinion. So the best we can do is push in the direction of our own personal opinion, knowing all the while that this is most likely not the true direction we want to go.

PUSHING THE BOULDER

How can this make any sense? Imagine a game where there is a large boulder that a group of people must push into a hole in the ground. The catch is that nobody knows the location of the hole. Each person can make their own educated guess but nobody knows for sure. The first person starts to push on the boulder. It barely moves. Then a second person starts to push, but in a slightly different direction. Then a third joins, pushing in yet another direction. All of the various force vectors from all the individual people pushing in different directions adds up to a single larger force vector in a single new direction—the trigonometric average of all the individual force vectors. It is that total force vector which is able to eventually find the hole. Why is this so? It seems quite random. Perhaps the universe or fate or karma or God waits to see that everyone is acting as they should, honestly representing their opinion, pushing as hard as they can, allowing others to push as well, and then simply moves the hole into the collective path of the new summed force vector. Perhaps in a wisdom-of-the-crowd event, the summed force vector actually is more correct as it utilizes the summed knowledge of all the people pushing, harnessing the combined brain power of the entire group which will always result in a truer outcome than if only a single brain had been used. Either way, it is important to notice that although the boulder as a whole is moving in the right direction, from any one individual's perspective it appears that the boulder is moving in a direction different from where they personally are pushing. Yet each person must realize that they want, indeed need, for this to be so. The direction of motion of the boulder is supposed to be different from where they are pushing. Said another way, each person is supposed to be pushing the boulder slightly off course. That cognitive dissonance is what makes it so difficult. It is not so easy to push in the direction you think you want and at the same time realize that you actually don't want that direction at all.

In the language of our previous discussion, the combined force vector representing the eventual motion of the boulder is the Actual Path and the hole toward which we are aiming is the TBD. When all is done correctly and honestly as in the previous discussion about the cherubs on the ark cover, then the individual opinions (individual force vectors in our current example) sum to an Actual Path (the combined force vector of the boulder) which leads to the TBD (the hole in the ground toward which we are aiming).

A WORD ABOUT AVERAGES

Both the image of the cherubs on the ark cover and the boulder analogy rely on the use of mathematical averages. In the case of the ark cover, the midpoint between the two cherubs is the exact average between the two extremes. In the boulder analogy, the summed force vector which results in the overall motion of the boulder is an exact mathematical average of all of the individual force vectors. But is it really this simple? If you find yourself thinking that this entire theory just boils down to a bunch of averages and is therefore too simplistic, please do not misunderstand these examples. Going back to the first decision-making theory from chapter 1, that between husband and wife, the TBD is not in every case the simple average between the two positions. Rather, it sometimes agrees with the husband's opinion, sometimes the wife's, and sometimes it may exist somewhere between the two or even outside the bounds of either's opinion. When we enlarge the decision-making process to include many more people, a similar logic applies. The TBD does not have to be a simple average defined somehow by summing all the opinions and dividing by their total number. A more colloquial use of the word average may be more apt, in that all the opinions taken together will indeed lead to the Actual Path which we hope will be close to the TBD. We might argue that in real life, weighted averages are used rather than simple averages, where some opinions are weighted more strongly than others, with the important caveat that we do not know the values of the relative weights. How does this work? Clearly it does not mean that some people can choose to weight their own opinions more highly than others. Instead, the weighting occurs naturally as part of the democratic process. Those opinions which are more compelling will by nature acquire more followers. Those opinions which have proven track records will perhaps be more compelling. But the relative weighting occurs as a consequence of more than just the strength or popularity of each opinion. There are often a host of external factors which affect the eventual outcome and which have little to do with the initial set of opinions. The result of the mixing and interaction of all the opinions coming together with each other and with new and changing external factors will by itself cause different weights to be assigned to different opinions such that the eventual Actual Path can not be predicted in advance as simply the exact mid-point between my opinion and your opinion, between Democrat and Republican, between progressive Democrat and Blue Dog Democrat, or between moderate Republican and MAGA Republican.

The point of the boulder analogy is not, therefore, that the Actual Path or the TBD can be calculated in advance as some average mid-point between everyone's opinions. The analogy does illustrate, however, that we each must be aware that the goal of our collective striving is to arrive at the TBD which may be different than our own opinion and that therefore the "direction" we are pushing may be different than the "direction" of the TBD (but that if we all push together we will eventually get there). It also illustrates the point that each of us has a responsibility to push in the direction our conscious leads us. What does this mean? It means being true to your own opinion and not simply following others. Everyone needs to push in their own direction in order for the summed, weighted force vector to result in the correct path. If one demagogue were to arise and a large segment of the population were to simply start pushing in the same direction as the demagogue instead of in their own individual directions, it would alter the course of the boulder. Does this occur in real life? Clearly in the case of popular demagogues it may. But this can occur at a much more subtle level whenever individuals outsource their thought to someone else.

OUTSOURCING THOUGHT

To explain the concept of outsourcing thought I would like to start with a few examples from health care. As a physician, I am constantly faced with the challenge of recommending the correct treatment plan for my patients. Doctors must gather information and make informed decisions which will affect the health of the people they treat. This information is often incomplete, the treatment options are often only partially successful, and many treatment options confer some degree of risk to the patient. In order to help doctors make these decisions, medical specialty societies have promulgated medical guidelines in an attempt to standardize what are considered to be the best practices in each field. However, these guidelines should only be used as recommendations and not as ironclad rules. Nevertheless, use of these guidelines has permeated all aspects of healthcare, to the point that they sometimes can begin to supplant personal thought and judgement.

A few years ago I received a call from the emergency department (ED) about a patient of mine who was there with atypical chest pain. The emergency physician was very capable and had been in practice for many years. He said to me, "Dr. Brodsky, your patient is here with chest pain. The pain is clearly atypical, the electrocardiogram is a little abnormal but is unchanged from prior, and the lab tests are negative. I do not think this is cardiac pain. Unfortunately our ED has begun using a new protocol for chest pain utilizing the 'heart score' and because of this patient's heart score I am forced to admit him to the observation unit." He was clearly uneasy as he was forced to follow a guideline that resulted in a decision that, while possibly not doing any harm in this case (the patient was uneventfully discharged the next day), was clearly not the correct medical decision for this patient and went against the judgement of both myself and the ED physician, both of whom felt that the patient could have been safely discharged from the ED.

In another example, I was rounding with my resident some time ago and I was explaining to him the reasoning we use to decide whether to use a certain blood thinning medication in a specific case. The case in question involved a patient who had been admitted with mild gastrointestinal bleeding and we presumed that the small heart-related lab elevation was not from a typical heart attack caused by blocked arteries, and therefore would not require the blood thinning medication. When the resident asked me point blank when I would use this medication and when I wouldn't, I half-jokingly referred him to the 1966 movie *Fantastic Voyage*.[3] After he looked it up on his smart phone, I told him that he needs to imagine that he is in that submarine, floating thru the patient's arteries, and when he gets to the patient's coronaries, he needs to look at them out the window of the little submarine. If he sees a blockage, then the patient needs the medication. If not, then they probably don't need it. Obviously there's more to the story, but for teaching purposes I wanted him to begin to think of the patho-physiology occurring in the patient's body rather than just look at numbers on the computer. So then the resident looked up at me and said, somewhat quizzically, "You mean it's just judgement?" As if to say, you mean there's no score I can look at? No guideline to tell me what to do? The resident apparently found it odd that he might have to use his judgement rather than outsource his thought to a guideline or protocol.

3. Fleischer, *Fantastic Voyage*.

One final example occurred when I was presented with a case by a fourth-year fellow about a patient who was admitted recently. The details are unimportant but suffice it to say that due to a rather arbitrary and probably inappropriate initial triage decision, the patient was routed through a series of guidelines and clinical pathways. This caused that patient to receive an unnecessary procedure and several unnecessary medications. The initial incorrect decision, though retrospectively incorrect, is not the point. These things happen, even if everything is done to the best of our abilities. What was more interesting and more unfortunate was that there were multiple opportunities for the physicians involved to change the course of their treatment strategy, however no change was ever made. Why? Because once a guideline has been selected it becomes very difficult to change course. A certain mental inertia is created making any deviation from that guideline very unlikely. In a way, those guidelines give physicians an excuse to stop thinking, to stop making decisions, and to stop using their judgement. We tell ourselves that we have no choice, that we must follow the guideline, seldom wondering whether the guideline may have been misapplied in the first place.

Each of these stories shows an example of physicians outsourcing their own thought to a guideline. The emergency room doctor in the first example was forced to defer to a guideline even though he felt in his gut that it was inappropriate. The medical resident in the second example had been socialized to expect that there would always be a guideline to follow, allowing him to avoid having to use his own judgement. The treating physicians in the third example failed to realize that a guideline had been misapplied and therefore plodded on with inappropriate treatments because they were unwilling or unable to use their own judgement to challenge the current guideline-directed treatment plan.

These examples show the allure and the pitfalls of an overreliance on guidelines to the exclusion of our own thoughtful judgement. Why do such things occur? Why do highly intelligent doctors succumb so easily to such scenarios? To understand this we must first understand why there are guidelines in the first place. Medical guidelines are written by medical specialty societies to take into account all of the latest research. They are typically updated every few years as new research becomes available. They are useful in fields where there is a vast amount of information to be learned which changes frequently. In such a case it can be very difficult for each doctor to maintain up-to-date knowledge about every single area within their scope of practice. Guidelines make it easier to know what to do without having to read through all the individual research papers yourself. When used properly these guidelines can be very helpful. But the guidelines can also become a crutch, lulling doctors into a false sense of security. Such a guideline culture can lead to bad outcomes if doctors are not constantly vigilant, using their own judgment along with, and in some cases even against, whatever the current guideline may be.

How is this related to American society at large today? I see parallels between the use of medical guidelines and the use of political platforms and talking points by both political parties today. Just like the vast amount of knowledge and research that is required of doctors, there is a vast amount of information about most political policy decisions, including research, polling data, economic data, position papers, etc. There is so much information that it is almost impossible for even good honest citizens to keep abreast of it all. Just as doctors rely on guidelines in those situations, published by their medical specialty societies, American citizens rely on party platforms published by their preferred political parties in order to help them make informed political decisions. When used appropriately these platforms can be useful. However, when accepted wholesale without any further thought, effectively outsourcing our own thought to political parties, then not only can bad outcomes occur, such as can occur in medicine, but we lose the thoughtful debate which makes our system work in the first place. When all thinking is concentrated in the minds of a few party members who make policy decisions and the rest blindly follow the published talking points, then the quality of our decision-making suffers greatly, as we discussed in the boulder analogy above.

This has become so common that when there arises a political figure who stays true to their honest opinions they tend to stick out like a sore thumb. Take, for example, the late Arizona senator John McCain. Senator McCain was a Republican senator who voted with the Republican party most of the time but was not afraid to vote with the opposition from time to time. For this, he was branded a "maverick" (a label of which he was proud), underscoring just how strange it was to have a senator who actually did not vote with his party every single time. Senator McCain is thus one of the exceptions which unfortunately proves the rule.

We collectively need our various tribes, parties, special interest groups, political affiliations, and individual opinions to keep pushing honestly in their own individual directions while we collectively wait with baited breath to see where it all leads. This means that we must allow the cognitive dissonance to remain ever-present between where we are pushing and where we are going. It means that we allow ourselves the luxury of pursing our personal beliefs while at the same time reveling in the pleasant surprise of the unexpected outcome of our collective national striving, knowing that it is taking us where we need to be.

MORE ON LISTENING

The part about listening to others is critically important, even if it sounds like an obvious cliche. In the shared decision-making model the husband and wife arrive at the Actual Path which hopefully leads to the TBD through debate, through each one standing "against" the other. But this only works if in addition to standing up for their own opinions they each listen to the opinions of the other. While it may not be too difficult for husbands and wives to listen to each other, when we apply this theory to the realm of politics it becomes increasing clear that listening to the other side is a much taller order. For a variety of reasons, several of which we discussed earlier, many in politics get caught up in their own views and are not really interested in what anyone else has to say. Once they have internalized the talking points of their chosen party, a sense of complacency sets in whereby they no longer wish to assimilate any new information or seek to understand any other opinions. Rather, they simply want to act on their own internalized convictions (and perhaps convince others to do the same). There is a classic story in the Bible which deals with this very difficult aspect of listening despite being convinced that we already know what has to be done. It is a very well-known story, one with which you may be familiar, though you may not have thought about it in quite this way. The story of which I am speaking is commonly called the binding of Isaac, and I would like to relate this particular teaching in the name of Rav[4] Mike Feuer, from whom I first heard this interpretation. The text of the story is as follows:

ויהי אחר הדברים האלה והאלקים נסה את אברהם ויאמר אליו אברהם ויאמר הנני: ויאמר קח נא את בנך את יחידך אשר אהבת את יצחק ולך לך אל ארץ המריה והעלהו שם לעלה על אחד ההרים אשר אמר אליך: וישכם אברהם בבקר ויחבש את חמרו ויקח את שני נעריו אתו ואת יצחק בנו ויבקע עצי עלה ויקם וילך אל המקום אשר אמר לו האלקים: ביום השלישי וישא אברהם את עיניו וירא את המקום מרחק: ויאמר אברהם אל נעריו שבו לכם פה עם החמור ואני והנער נלכה עד כה ונשתחוה ונשובה אליכם: ויקח אברהם את עצי העולה וישם על יצחק בנו ויקח בידו את האש ואת המאכלת <u>וילכו שניהם יחדו</u>: ויאמר יצחק אל אברהם אביו ויאמר אבי ויאמר הנני בני ויאמר הנה האש והעצים ואיה השה לעלה: ויאמר אברהם אלקים יראה לו השה לעלה בני <u>וילכו שניהם יחדו</u>: ויבאו אל המקום אשר אמר לו האלקים ויבן שם אברהם את המזבח ויערך את העצים ויעקד את יצחק בנו וישם אתו על המזבח ממעל לעצים: וישלח אברהם את ידו ויקח את המאכלת לשחט את בנו: ויקרא אליו מלאך יקוק מן השמים ויאמר אברהם אברהם ויאמר הנני: ויאמר אל תשלח ידך אל הנער ואל תעש לו מאומה כי עתה ידעתי כי ירא אלקים אתה ולא חשכת את בנך את יחידך ממני: וישא אברהם את עיניו וירא והנה איל אחר נאחז בסבך בקרניו וילך אברהם ויקח את האיל ויעלהו לעלה תחת בנו:

Vayhi achar haddevarim ha'elleh veha'elohim nissah et-avraham vayyomer elav avraham vayyomer hinneni. Vayyomer kach-na et-bincha et-yechidcha asher-ahavta

4. "Rav" is a commonly used Hebrew contraction of the title "Rabbi."

*et-yitzchak velech-lecha el-eretz hammoriyyah veha'alehu
sham le'olah al achad heharim asher omar eleicha.
Vayyashkem avraham babboker vayyachavosh et-cham-
oro vayyikkach et-shenei ne'arav itto ve'et yitzchak beno
vayvakka atzei olah vayyakom vayyelech el-hammakom
asher-amar-lo ha'elohim. Bayyom hashelishi vayyissa
avraham et-einav vayyar et-hammakom merachok. Vayyomer avraham el-ne'arav shevu-lachem poh im-hachamor
va'ani vehanna'ar nelechah ad-koh venishtachaveh ve-
nashuvah aleichem. Vayyikkach avraham et-atzei ha'olah
vayyasem al-yitzchak beno vayyikkach beyado et-ha'esh
ve'et-hamma'achelet <u>vayyelechu sheneihem yachdav.</u> Vayyomer yitzchak el-avraham aviv vayyomer avi vayyomer
hinnenni veni vayyomer hinneh ha'esh veha'etzim ve'ayyeh
hasseh le'olah. Vayyomer avraham elohim yir'eh-lo hasseh
le'olah beni <u>vayyelechu sheneihem yachdav.</u> Vayyavo'u
el-hammakom asher amar-lo ha'elohim vayyiven sham
avraham   et-hammizbeach   vayya'aroch   et-ha'etzim
vayya'akod et-yitzchak beno vayyasem oto al-hammiz-
beach mimma'al la'etzim. Vayyishlach avraham et-yado
vayyikkach et-hamma'achelet lishchot et-beno. Vayyikra
elav mal'ach adonai min-hashamayim vayyomer avraham avraham vayyomer hinneni. Vayyomer al-tishlach
yadecha el-hanna'ar ve'al-ta'as lo me'umah ki attah yada'ti
ki-yere elohim attah velo chasachta et-bincha et-yechidcha
mimmenni. Vayyissa avraham et-einav vayyar vehinneh-
ayil achar ne'echaz bassevach bekarnav vayyelech avraham vayyikkach et-ha'ayil vayya'alehu le'olah tachat beno.*

Some time afterward, God put Abraham to the test. He
said to him, "Abraham," and he answered, "Here I am."
And He said, "Take your son, your favored one, Isaac,
whom you love, and go to the land of Moriah, and offer
him there as a burnt offering on one of the heights that I
will point out to you." So early next morning, Abraham
saddled his ass and took with him two of his servants
and his son Isaac. He split the wood for the burnt offering, and he set out for the place of which God had told
him. On the third day Abraham looked up and saw the
place from afar. Then Abraham said to his servants, "You
stay here with the ass. The boy and I will go up there; we

will worship and we will return to you." Abraham took the wood for the burnt offering and put it on his son Isaac. He himself took the firestone and the knife; <u>and the two walked off together.</u> Then Isaac said to his father Abraham, "Father!" And he answered, "Yes, my son." And he said, "Here are the firestone and the wood; but where is the sheep for the burnt offering?" And Abraham said, "God will see to the sheep for His burnt offering, my son." <u>And the two of them walked on together</u>. They arrived at the place of which God had told him. Abraham built an altar there; he laid out the wood; he bound his son Isaac; he laid him on the altar, on top of the wood. And Abraham picked up the knife to slay his son. Then an angel of the Lord called to him from heaven: "Abraham! Abraham!" And he answered, "Here I am." And he said, "Do not raise your hand against the boy, or do anything to him. For now I know that you fear God, since you have not withheld your son, your favored one, from Me." When Abraham looked up, his eye fell upon a ram, caught in the thicket by its horns. So Abraham went and took the ram and offered it up as a burnt offering in place of his son.[5]

This is a difficult story. Many commentaries have been written about its meaning and purpose, ranging from simple historical theories about how the ancient practice of child sacrifice was banned by the progenitors of the early Israelites, to more philosophical discussions about the nature of obedience, to difficult questions about the very nature of God and humanity. I am not a rabbi and my purpose here is not to undertake an in-depth study of these verses. However, the interpretation which was shared with me is very interesting and is directly relevant to the topics of this book.

When most of us read this story our initial reaction to the second verse, the one in which God tells Abraham to sacrifice his son Isaac, is one of sheer horror. Just the thought of being told to sacrifice your child is so utterly abhorrent that we can hardly even conceive of such a thing. Yet most of us know that child sacrifice

5. Gen 22:1–13, translation from *Tanakh: The Holy Scriptures*.

was indeed practiced during those times. Even so, we can imagine that such a thing would never have been easy and would likely have required much psychological training and preparation. Lest you think such a thing does not exist today, an unthinkable act which requires much psychological training in order to accomplish, witness the modern phenomenon of suicide bombers. In those horrifying cases, a person chooses to actively kill themselves in the service of a perceived higher calling. Even if this is not exactly the same thing as ancient child sacrifice, it is a practice which goes against the basic human instinct for self-preservation and therefore requires a lengthy time of intense psychological training in order to put one's self into the correct frame of mind to be able to carry out such a difficult act. If we think of the participants in the biblical story not as simple one dimensional cartoon characters but rather as real human beings with real emotions, we can perhaps read between the lines to see what must have been going on in their minds.

Undoubtedly, Abraham would have been stunned at the request and it would have required some time for him to process the gravity of the task. It is therefore worth noting that the text specifically mentions that God chose a place which was a three day journey away, so that Abraham would have time to mentally prepare himself. We can only guess what must have been going through Abraham's mind during those three days. We know that he was close to God, that he trusted God, and that he had already had several experiences with God, including even arguing with God over the fate of the ultimately destroyed cities of Sodom and Gomorrah.[6] It is instructive to note that Abraham chose not to argue with God in this particular instance. We do not know why. Perhaps the sheer horrifying enormity of the task was too overwhelming, or perhaps it just seemed too self-serving to argue with God about something in which he obviously had such a personal vested interest. Whatever the reason, he must have worked very hard to mentally condition himself.

6. Gen 18:23–33.

In reading the biblical verses there is actually a textual hint alluding to this fact. What is this hint? Remember, the Bible uses words sparingly. Whenever words or phrases are repeated there is often a hidden meaning. When Abraham and Isaac arrive at the site of the sacrifice, they gather their tools and set out, leaving their servants behind. The text then says, "and the two walked off together." Almost immediately, Isaac asks where is the sheep for the sacrifice. Abraham responds that God will provide the sheep. Then it says once again, "and the two of them walked on together." The English translation uses a slightly different wording each time though the meaning is the same. The original Hebrew it is more striking because the words are exactly the same each time: "וילכו שניהם יחדו—*vayyelechu sheneihem yachdav*" (underlined in the text above).

The image of a father and son walking together is a very peaceful image. Further, most interpretations assume that Isaac himself was an adult at this point while Abraham was quite old. It is clear then, that the entire episode could not have occurred without Isaac's consent. If it is not clear whether Isaac knew about the plan initially, the ambiguity of Abraham's answer to Isaac's question ("God will provide the sheep") followed by the repeated image of the two of them walking on together leaves little doubt that Isaac must have known by then, and therefore must have been at peace with the idea himself.

It is also worth noting specifically where this repeated phrase is not used. At the beginning of the journey, before the three days had elapsed, the text could have said something similar about how they all set off together, or they started walking together, or some such parallel peaceful sentiment. Yet it doesn't. Only after the three days have elapsed do we see this peaceful image, and then not once but twice. Clearly something happened during those three days which resulted in such a dreadful peacefulness. I do not mean to say that there was some missing physical experience during the journey, only that Abraham must have used the time to meditate or pray or think or otherwise prepare himself such that he was able

to become completely transformed into someone at peace with his
mission, able to carry out the difficult task required.

MENTAL INERTIA

I have had occasion to witness, while not exactly the same state
of mind, perhaps something similar in my medical practice. As a
cardiologist, I routinely treat patients with heart failure. Most of
the time we are successful at dramatically improving the quality
of life for these patients through a combination of medications,
minimally invasive catheter-based interventions, and occasion-
ally surgical intervention. Rarely, however, a patient progresses
to what we call end-stage heart failure, perhaps combined with
other difficult non-cardiac illnesses, where we have reached the
limits of what modern medicine can offer. At those trying times,
as part of my practice I have sometimes been there as patients unfortunately take their last steps from this world and into the next.
Sometimes this occurs suddenly and unexpectedly. In that case the
patient may have no time to mentally prepare; the rapidity of the
illness and subsequent passing is simply too fast. Sometimes there
is time for the family and loved ones to prepare themselves while
the patient lies unaware, medically incapacitated by the disease
itself or due to the effect of sedative medications often used in that
setting. Sometimes the patient themself, while still living at home
and of sound mind and body, knows that the end is approaching.
They have spent a great deal of time thinking about their life, the
loved ones they will leave behind, the ending of their journey in
this world; and they eventually come to a sort of peace with their
impending death.

So far, you may notice that nothing I have described seems in
any way out of the ordinary, unexpected, or otherwise improper.
But once in a great while I will see a patient such as this, one who
has endured the necessary time and mental energy in coming to
terms with their approaching death, and yet, when I look at their
medical history and condition, I find that there is actually quite a
bit that can be done to improve the quality of their life and prolong

its duration. I am not speaking of large, invasive surgeries or incapacitating chemotherapy drugs, but simply "regular" medications that a person can take once or twice a day, without any side effects, and which could have a significant impact on improving the function of their heart and therefore the quality of their life. Most often when patients come to me suffering from heart failure, they are quite happy to hear that with relatively simple maneuvers (such as easy-to-take pills) we can dramatically improve their well-being. However, when a patient has expended such a great amount of mental energy that they are able to finally come to peace with their assumed impending death, the mental inertia which is created can be so overwhelming as to be totally paralyzing. I have had a few patients who have been simply unable to deal with the fact that their condition is simply not as bad as they had been led to believe. They are so mentally invested in their approaching demise, that they are totally unable to process the information that with a few simple pills they could have their life back. Because these patients are mentally competent and are able to make their own decisions, they are free to refuse treatment. I have watched, with great heartbreak, as a few patients of mine have ultimately passed away when I am certain they could have had at least several more enjoyable years of life. I want to stress that what is strange about these few cases is not that these patients were refusing treatment because they were morally opposed to the treatment (in the way that some are opposed to using blood products, for example), because they were opposed to the unbearable side effects of the treatment (common with some chemotherapies for cancer, for example), or because their current quality of life was so bad as to not be worth living (common with the unbearable air-hunger experienced by end stage emphysema patients, for example). No, these patients would have no problem taking the pills we have to offer them, were it not for the fact that they simply had convinced themselves that they were dying.

How is this related to the Abraham story above? Just like these patients, Abraham (and perhaps Isaac as well) was able to mentally condition himself to be at peace with an approaching dreadful experience. Just like these patients, one would expect that there might be a significant amount of mental inertia invested in that mental state. It is here that we must notice another interesting point about the biblical narration. In the beginning of the story it is God who speaks to Abraham, asking him to sacrifice his son Isaac. However, who is it at the end of the story that finally tells Abraham not to slay his son? If you look carefully, you will see that it is not God, but "an angel of the Lord." Lest you say, "Who cares? It's basically the same thing," or "If God spoke to me or if an angel spoke to me, my response would be no different," I remind you that the Bible uses words sparingly and selectively. If God and the angels in heaven are basically the same thing, then why not use parallel language throughout the story? Why specifically say God in one place and an angel in another?

Let's put ourselves back into the mind of Abraham. He has mentally prepared himself and is at peace with the upcoming dreadful act he must do, as requested by God. He must know this is some kind of test, and with his supreme faith he is willing to see it through. Then, suddenly, he hears a voice—not God—telling him exactly the opposite of what God told him earlier. How would you respond? If you are like the patients who have not entirely given up hope and are therefore overjoyed to hear that their life can still be saved, then perhaps you would jump at the opportunity to avoid the approaching catastrophic act. But what if you were like the patients who have entirely given up any hope of living, having come to peace even with death itself, and for whom it is simply impossible to change course? Like those patients who are unable to listen to the physician offering them a way to avoid their own death, might you also not be able to stop yourself from seeing through the task at hand?

Had God been the one to tell Abraham to stop, he would have had no choice, for we would surely not expect Abraham to disobey a direct order from God. But an angel? Could not the mental inertia have been strong enough to convince him that maybe the angel is just an illusion; his subconscious playing tricks on him in a last ditch effort to avoid the completion of the task? Abraham is strong.

He is mentally prepared. He knows what he must do. He has been preparing for three days. What would you do?

Here we see the true miracle in this interpretation of the story. The miracle is that Abraham was still able to listen. The text itself testifies to the enormity of the act. When the angel tells Abraham not to harm his son, it doesn't simply move from the angel's request to the staying of Abraham's hand followed by the sacrifice of the ram caught in the thicket. Rather, it dwells, somewhat awkwardly even, on that specific moment of listening. The angel cries out, "Abraham, Abraham," at which point Abraham does nothing except listen, responding simply with "הנני—*hinneni*—here I am." Only then does the angel follow with the request not to harm the boy.

We have seen that word before, "הנני—*hinneni*—here I am." It is the same word used when Abraham first heard God's call in the very first verse of the story. In fact, that word is often used when God calls to a person and the person recognizes the call, presenting themself for divine service. It is perhaps easy to understand a person being open to hearing God's call, the initial state of receiving one's mission, the openness of mind which comes with the realization that one is beginning a new course. But it is perhaps not so common for a person, after having fully internalized their perceived mission, to retain the ability to listen wholeheartedly once again, resulting in a 180-degree change of course.

Do not think this is easy. Yes, Abraham was able to keep listening when the angel called. But let us look carefully at how the story ends. We all know that at the end of the story Abraham ends up sacrificing the ram instead of his son. Let us consider what might have been in the mind of Abraham at that moment. If we assume the typical viewpoint, that Abraham was loath to sacrifice his son and was happy to be offered a way out, then we would expect him to celebrate that moment. We might expect him to see the ram, sacrifice it, and partake of the meat with his son and even with the rest of his retinue in a festive atmosphere as he basked in the euphoria of having been spared his beloved son. But he doesn't do that. Or perhaps a bit more stoically, we might expect him to see the ram, and sacrifice it as a simple thanksgiving offering to God for saving the life of his son. But he doesn't do that either. No, the text says specifically that he offered up the ram "as a burnt offering in place of his son." If you read carefully you will notice two things: First, Abraham is offering up the ram not as a thanksgiving offering but as a burnt offering—exactly the kind of offering he was told to make of his son. Second, he offers up that burnt offering specifically in place of his son. It is as if the mental inertia which had built up was too great to simply vanish of its own accord. Rather, even after listening to the angel telling him not to harm his son, he had so conditioned himself to complete the ghastly task that he simply could not just let it go. Instead, he used the ram as a way to vent his mental inertia—as a way of allowing himself to complete the task, albeit without harming his son. So yes, Abraham was able to listen and to continue listening right up until the end, as should we. But the text makes no illusions as to the great difficulty this type of listening presents.

That is perhaps a different way to read the story than what you have heard before. Typically, we think of Abraham dreading the act he must do and we assume he would be seeking any opportunity at all to avoid it altogether. But with a more careful reading and an eye toward the capacity of the human mind to build up immense mental inertia, we see the exact opposite: that sometimes the hardest thing for a person to do is to continue listening. Part of the greatness of Abraham is that in always listening he was able to keep his mind open so that he would be ever ready to heed the divine call, even when it meant so abruptly changing directions.

MODERN COLLECTIVE NON-LISTENING

How does this relate to us, today? The biblical story of Abraham and the binding of Isaac, and the rare patients I have described who are unable to change course when facing their own death, are extreme examples where the mind can become locked in place, unable to consider any other alternatives. But I would hazard a guess that you have noticed people around you who appear to be similarly locked into a certain path, a certain mental framework, to the exclusion of all others. If we look at political discourse today, when politically minded people have "figured things out" and "know what must be done," all that remains then is to complete the task.

Let's consider two modern examples of what happens when people stop listening and simply drone on ahead without any regard to other opinions. The first example is the response to the second-wave COVID-19 resurgence in parts of the United States in the fall of 2020. Two opinions regarding what to do were circulating during that time: one suggested sacrificing the economy in order to save as many lives as possible through a second round of lockdowns and closures; the other suggesting sacrificing some of the ill elderly in order to save the economy (by avoiding economically damaging closures which may have resulted in downstream morbidity or even mortality from loss of jobs, income, healthcare, etc.). While each of us can make our own educated guess as to which opinion we prefer, did any of us know for sure which would really be better in the end? Clearly, the answer is no. We were all just guessing. We are a representative democracy and have elected leaders and appointees whom we have chosen to make such decisions. What ought to have happened is that there should have been public discourse about the issue for a time, but once a decision was made by our elected representatives or by their appointees everyone should have accepted that decision. That's not to say that everyone should have agreed with the decision. Clearly disagreement will continue. However, as Americans who believe in representative democracy as the best way for a nation to reach complex decisions, one can at the same time maintain one's own opinion and yet go along with the decision which the democratic process has produced—the Actual Path in our previous discussion. After all, who really knew what the best approach was anyway? Most of the arguments on either side were only speculative. The logical thing to do was to engage in rigorous debate, but then to rally around whatever the final decision turned out to be.

The initial arguments in the above COVID-19 debate centered around liberal news outlets wanting to use masking, social distancing, and delaying opening up the economy in order to stop the virus while conservative news outlets wanted to open up the economy faster, putting less emphasis on measures to stop the virus. Soon, however, the argument shifted such that the conservative news outlets accused the liberals of wanting to harm the economy purposefully because a bad economy would help them in the presidential election later that fall. The liberal news outlets in turn accused the conservatives of only caring about money and the economy even if people were dying, etc. Thus the discussion morphed into a fight over motives, each side ascribing hate, rage, dishonesty, etc., to the other, all the while employing those same tactics themselves because they felt they had no choice. Each side saw the situation as life or death, reinforcing the delusion that they had no choice but to fight back as hard as possible. In such a life or death fight there can be no compromise. This occurred as the discussion shifted from the actual problem of what to do about COVID-19, which was not very clear or obvious, to unrelated arguments about motives, which were easier to understand and more extreme.

However it only takes a minute to zoom back out from that raging fight over motives to see that the original issue was not the evil motives of the other side, or how they can't be trusted to make decisions because all they care about is getting their people elected, or whatever the most extreme arguments were at the time. The original issue was how best to deal with the coronavirus, and neither option was very good (either sacrificing the economy which could result in downstream morbidity or even mortality, versus directly sacrificing some elderly in order to prevent such downstream damage). After a short time arguing these new, more extreme arguments, most people had forgotten what the original issue was in the first place. After all, it was much more fun to be hurling insults at each other and berating the ulterior motives of the other side than to be dealing with a complex problem with no clear right answer anyway. There we have a perfect example of two bleeding extremist camps facing off against each other, each unwilling to listen to the other. By impugning their motives, each side was not willing to grant the other any legitimacy whatsoever. Neither side was interested in listening to the other as can be seen by the fact that the arguments made by each side had nothing to do with the stated position of their adversary.

Further examples of this phenomenon are found in the political arguments surrounding the immigration debate. Immigration has been a political issue for many years. It is a complex topic with many moving parts, including border security; policy and process relating to the legal pathway for foreign nationals to apply for and obtain US citizenship; the humanitarian crisis related to asylum seekers coming from countries with violent political instability; the humanitarian crisis related to undocumented illegal aliens who already exist and live in our country; and the humanitarian issues related to children born in the US of undocumented parents who are living in the US in contravention of US immigration laws. All of these issues have shaped the political debate surrounding immigration policy for decades. However, recently the debate has changed. Instead of arguing about immigration policy itself, the political extremes on either end have begun to change the argument to one involving the insincere and egregiously evil motives of the other side. For example, Republicans have posited that Democrats do not really care about any so-called humanitarian crisis. Rather, their real purpose is to wholesale remake American demographics by importing vast numbers of illegal aliens who are likely to vote Democratic, therefore securing Democratic rule for decades into the future. This argument does not have anything to do with what a reasonable immigration policy might look like, which would be a complicated topic to discuss. Rather, it is an argument against the perceived motives of the other side. It is a useful argument in that it posits an extreme, dishonest, and indeed evil motive to the other side. If you cannot understand or are not interested in actual immigration policy, surely you will be motived by the contemptible evil motives of the other side. The Democrats argue the same thing in reverse; that by disallowing anyone into the country who will not vote Republican and who is not "racially pure," the Republicans are using immigration policy only as a tool to strengthen their white supremacist ideology. The debate has thus been shifted away from the actual policy itself toward a simple rant about the evil motives of the other side.

Again, it only takes a minute to zoom back out and see that "the wholesale remaking of American voting demography" and "the supporting of white supremacist ideology" have very little to do with crafting a complicated solution to the complicated problem of immigration policy. They are, however, quite extreme ideas which are easy to understand and easy to argue against, which quite unfortunately is exactly the point. Neither side is actually interested in listening to what the other has to say, but instead wants to craft their own fake adversary against whom it is easier to argue.

The ossified finality of such a mental state, when one is so convinced of their own correctness that they are totally unwilling to even listen to any other opinions, can be at the same time a lazy capitulation to political talking points, a self-affirming psychological certainty requiring total obedience, and a frightening battle to the death for one's own chosen path lest the entire project be lost if one fails and any of the "wrong" alternatives ever come to fruition. But it is exactly there, in the ideally never-ending act of listening, as we charge headlong into the too-often extreme paths we have chosen, that we must remember the existence of a TBD, a Theoretically Better Decision, a God's-eye view, that is always unknowable yet always calling to us, as the angel called to Abraham. No matter how invested we are in our own opinions, no matter if our entire sense of self-worth is built upon our winning political battles, if we cannot admit to ourselves that because we do not have knowledge of the TBD we must always keep listening, then we are consigned by our own hand to the divisiveness and polarization rampant in our country today.

Chapter Three

Forces of Unity

If we look at American history since the Civil War, we see that the post–Civil War Reconstruction Era ended only a single generation before the First World War. During this time the country was on a trajectory of reunification after the biggest crisis the country had ever faced. Following this, the First World War served to unite the country, and the country would soon be united once again by the Second World War. That "greatest generation" was united in purpose in the defeat of fascism and the liberation of Europe from Nazi tyranny. We Americans were the "good guys" who were fighting the "bad guys." It was just that simple. Following on the heels of the Second World War was the Cold War, during which the United States saw itself as the champion of freedom and democracy throughout the world. Despite the internal divisions that characterized the Vietnam and Korean wars and despite the civil unrest that appropriately shook America in the 1960s, the overall feeling that we were the global "good guys" fighting for democracy and justice was still a strong uniting factor holding American society together. Perhaps the divisiveness of 1960s race relations and the antiwar movements during the Vietnam years were somewhat countered by the sense of unity that the early space race offered—if we had gone off track regarding our role as world leader of democracy and freedom, at least we were leading the world into the technological revolution of the space age.

However, since the Cold War ended in the 1990s, there has not been anything to take its place in uniting Americans in purpose. There was perhaps a brief period of unity in the immediate aftermath of the terrorist attacks of September 11, 2001, however it was short-lived. There simply no longer exists an agreed upon existential enemy which we all face together. It was a thirty-year span between the end of the Reconstruction Era after the Civil War until the first World War, and it was approximately twenty years between the First and Second World Wars, leading directly into the Cold War. The Soviet Union dissolved in 1991 marking the end of the Cold War. That means that as of 2021, it has been more than thirty years since the last major conflict which has united the country. Beginning in 2022 the United States has been in uncharted territory with more time having elapsed since the last major external uniting crisis than ever before in our history since the Civil War. Perhaps we should dwell on that thought a bit longer. Thirty years is little more than a single generation. Going forward will be the first time since the Civil War that young adults taking on leadership roles in the country will have no firsthand knowledge of any time when the country was united by a common adversary.

Rather than uniting the country, our most serious foreign adversaries of today, Iran, Russia, and China, each serve as forces for division in our society, to say nothing of the COVID-19 pandemic which surprisingly and alarmingly has also only divided us further. America has been receding on the national stage as it mangled several attempts at democratic nation-building in the Middle East, apologized for it, pivoted to Asia, and then swung back to ourselves chanting "America first." This begs the question, other than ourselves what do we stand for? One has to ask if life, liberty, and the pursuit of happiness really cuts it anymore. Back in the early days of the United States that may have been enough—we were blazing a new trail in a new land with an entirely new form of government, crafted from scratch. It was a grand experiment and it worked. However, today that war has been won. Our country and our form of government is taken for granted and seems no longer sufficient to give us a common sense of purpose.

To be more concrete about it, life is obviously important—you need safety before anything else. Liberty is also important but is universally agreed to be so and is no longer unique to our country. What about the pursuit of happiness? While obviously good on the surface, we must consider the time period in which this phrase from the Declaration of Independence was written. Happiness at that time might have meant tending one's cherry orchard in peace without being bothered by heavy-handed taxation or by unethical and overbearing monarchs. Later, it may have incorporated the sense of rugged individualism one could find by building one's own home in a wide-open, new territory, unbothered by prying government officials. (Notwithstanding the fact that the the "wide-open territory" was in fact Native American land and many of the homes were built on the backs of African American slave labor—history is still history, even if ugly.) Today, however, if happiness is only defined by consumerism, if the overarching societal culture is one of capitalistic consumerism and nothing else, then happiness today is in danger of becoming a never-ending race in which we all compete against each other to acquire more material goods and social status. That competition acts as a divisive force. Without any other external uniting force such as has occurred in the past during wartime, the end result risks becoming simply a zero-sum, materialistic, consumer-oriented competition for limited resources among divided individuals.

This situation has led to an imbalance where the naturally divisive forces in our society are becoming stronger than anything which unites us. When seen in this light it becomes clear that the only solution can be to either diminish that which divides us, as we have discussed in the previous two chapters, or to find some other force or forces which could actively unite us.

ISRAEL AND AMERICA

In discussing what might act as a countering force to all of the disuniting forces inherent in our culture, I would like to look at the country of Israel as a case study. Perhaps as Americans wonder what, if anything, they have in common anymore, the US-Israel relationship can offer a reminder. If I were to ask you what's so special about the relationship between Israel and the United States, what would you say? If you're like most, you'll respond by saying that America is the main defender of democracy in the world, and that Israel, being the only democracy in the Middle East, is an important American ally. If you have a more religious bent you might point out that American values are founded on the Judeo-Christian ethic and that Israel shares those values. And while these statements may be true, neither of them are unique to America and neither gets at the root of the connection between the US and Israel.

Let's start with the fact that they are both democracies. Clearly there is nothing special about that because there are a lot of other democracies in the world—all of Europe, for example. The second reason is the Judeo-Christian ethic. Again, perhaps true, but then wouldn't it make more sense for Israel to have a special relationship with an actual Christian country, rather than the United States, a country specifically without an established religion? For example, Great Britain is an officially Christian state with the official state religion being the Anglican Church. So, as an actual Christian state, would not Britain share Israel's Judeo-Christian values even more than American would?

You might be tempted to admit that there may be no reason at all for Israel to be connected specifically with America; maybe it's only because the largest Jewish diaspora happens to be living in America. Maybe American Jews simply like pointing to these reasons (democracy and the Judeo-Christian ethic) even though they're no less true for other countries. Maybe because there are so many less Jews in other countries the story just sticks better as it relates to the United States. But is that really all there is? Let's examine what the American Israel Public Affairs Committee (AIPAC) has to say. This is a direct quote from their homepage:

> The U.S.-Israel relationship is a mutually beneficial partnership that reinforces America's moral values and strategic interests. America and Israel are sister democracies dedicated to the rule of law, human rights, and freedoms of speech and religion. The U.S.-Israel relationship is a key pillar of America's regional security framework. The Jewish state is a reliable, stable ally that advances American interests in a highly volatile and strategically important region of the world.[1]

This mission statement mentions both the "moral values" angle (the Judeo-Christian ethic mentioned earlier) and the democracy angle. The AIPAC statement showcases the US-Israel relationship in what I have heard described by Rabbi Yehuda HaKohen as a "Batman and Robin" style. In other words, Israel plays Robin to America's Batman. Israel is a "reliable, stable ally that advances American interests . . ." in the same way that Robin helps Batman accomplish his various crime-fighting tasks. It seems that even AIPAC agrees with the conventional wisdom that what ties Israel and America together is democracy and Judeo-Christian values.

THE KNIGHTS OF THE ROUND TABLE

But let's dig a little deeper. As opposed to most other Western democracies, the US does not have a history stretching back into antiquity and beyond. It does not have a mythic-historical cultural reference point which unites the country in the same way that Britain does, or France does, or Italy does, or Japan does. For example, in Winston Churchill's famous "We Shall Fight on the Beaches" speech during World War II, the following passage appears:

> The Knights of the Round Table, the Crusaders, all fall back into the past—not only distant but prosaic; these young men, going forth every morn to guard their native

1. "America & Israel: Connected for Good."

> land and all that we stand for, holding in their hands
> these instruments of colossal and shattering power. . .[2]

In Britain, the Knights of Round Table and the Crusaders are a mythic-historical cultural reference point stretching back a thousand years. When Churchill referenced those two cultural icons everyone in the United Kingdom knew what he was talking about; it touched a deep cultural chord in their society. However, such a thing does not exist in the United States. America is unlike just about every other Western democracy due to exactly that lack of collective, shared, premodern history. Unlike France or Britain, America was not already a country from time immemorial, which then, post-Enlightenment, transformed itself into a democracy. Rather uniquely in the world, America was instead founded post-Enlightenment only on a set of ideas.

Think about that for a moment, because people often forget just how strange that is. People not originally from here, came to America and created a new country based only on foundational ideas about human dignity and liberty (notwithstanding the disaster perpetrated on the Native Americans already living there and the experience with African slavery). Every other country just grew up where they had always been, with the people that had always been there. But not America. Because the United States is not just democracy and immigrants and melting pots. It's an idea about a better society.

One might point to other New World countries and wonder if they would not be subject to the same theory, however the United States is still unique for many reasons. First, most other countries in the New World were founded later than America, many not until the mid-nineteenth century. Second, many of the Latin American countries retain a much more dominant native cultural element to their modern populations which may serve to give them an older and stronger cultural identity. Third, many of them have had multiple, often violent, transitions between various forms, including monarchies, dictatorships, and republics, often

---

2. Churchill, "We Shall Fight on the Beaches."

in rapid succession, such that many modern New World countries today are quite young indeed and there is no singular thread of ideas which runs through all the historical iterations which came before. In the case of Canada, perhaps the most stable country in the New World other than the United States, it was only in 1982 that it became officially separate from Great Britain. Only the United States, then, retains its identity from its founding until the present, and only it therefore retains its founding ideas.

To be clear, this does not mean that other countries don't have ideas. *Liberté, égalité, fraternité* are the ideas upon which the French Republic was founded. One might therefore say that they have their ideas and we have ours and beyond that it doesn't matter. But when the French Republic was founded, the French people already existed—they already had a shared culture and a shared history which predated those ideas. Not so with the United States.

GUESS WHO ELSE?

Now that we have established the historical uniqueness of the United States of America, let us pause for a moment to see if we can think of any other country with a similar founding story. Let me make it more clear: can you think of an occasion when, at a time when there already existed many countries with long histories of their own, a group of people with barely any history, originally from somewhere else, came to a new land to found a new country based on new moral and ethical ideas? The answer is yes, and that country is Israel—the original, biblical Israel. We are used to thinking about ancient Israel originally as a family. Through this lens, Israel's origin story was simply that the Israelite family, starting with Abraham, grew into a nation in Egypt and then settled eventually in the promised land, as per God's plan.

But let's look at it through a different lens. At that time there were other major powers—Egypt, Babylon, Assyria, etc.—all of whom were each united by a common geography and a common history, similar to the other Western democracies of today—Britain, France, Italy, etc. And then along comes Israel, moves into a new land—Canaan—and sets up a new country not based on a long-standing, shared geographical, historical identity, but rather, based on the ideas contained in the Torah. True, Israel was born out of a single family with a shared destiny, but at that time it only stretched back several generations—much younger than any of the other surrounding empires. (The Torah counts only six generations between Abraham and Moses.) But just that shared destiny—just being family—wasn't enough. If it were, the Israelites would have left Egypt and gone directly to the promised land. But they didn't. They stopped at Mount Sinai. Because the new country was to be founded not on the basis of family or history alone, but on the basis of the ideas, ethics, and the system of governance outlined in the Torah. Even the modern State of Israel is composed of immigrants coming (back) together from different parts of the world in order to build (rebuild) a new (old) country based on specific ideals and values—similar to the story of the original American pilgrims.

So now it becomes clear. The unique relationship between the US and Israel is not some modern power play where the young Israeli Robin can aid the more established and wiser American Batman. Nor is it simply because they both happen to be democracies. It is because each country was founded specifically on a set of ideas about how human society can be better, and therefore as beacons of hope to the rest of the world. No other countries claim that origin story. If there is one idea from which all Americans should be able to draw inspiration, it should be that.

WHY ARE YOU AMERICAN?

If I were to ask most Americans, excluding recent immigrants, "Why are you American?" most would probably say, "Because I was born here," or "Because my family is here." Maybe for a country whose identity is based solely on the shared historical experience of lots of people having lived together in the same place for a long time, that would be enough. When the French Republic was formed, the people living there at the time probably would have answered the same. Very few people moved to France from somewhere else in the middle of the revolution because they wanted to create some new country based on *liberté, égalité* and *fraternité*. Rather, the people who were already living there were just trying to figure out how to govern themselves the best way they could. So while "because I was born here" or "because this is where my family is" might suffice for France, it seems America is beginning to discover that those answers do not suffice for a country based solely on ideas. While the early generations of American immigrants and pilgrims surely knew that—they were, after all, moving there for that reason—perhaps we today need to be reminded. Maybe the correct answer should be, "Because I believe in the ideas upon which America was founded." The fact that this might seem an unlikely thing for modern Americans to say highlights the exact problem that any idea-based country faces: the farther away it gets from its original founding, the more likely the population is to forget those original ideas. Paradoxically, the one group who might actually say something about American ideals as a reason for living in America might be recent immigrants, who have the outside perspective to appreciate just what America has to offer.

Compared to the United States, Israel is a very young country. But biblical Israel (and Judaism, its inheritor) is much older. It would be worthwhile for Americans to ask themselves how biblical Israel, or Judaism, has dealt with this issue. To understand this we must turn our attention to some aspects of Jewish ritual practice. One of the most central Jewish holidays is Passover, during which we Jews are commanded to tell our story of liberation. The concept is so central and powerful that we are commanded to tell the story in the first person, as if we ourselves were liberated from slavery. Further, there are remembrances of this story in the daily prayer liturgy, such that the message is repeated every day, all year. You see, Judaism and Israel knew that "because my family lives here" is not the right answer. They knew that the only answer that could work, that could sustain the people over the centuries and millennia, was "I believe in the ideas upon which the country was founded." In summary, there are two idea-based countries in the world: the United States and Israel. One of them has been around for millennia. One of them has been around for a mere 250 years and is currently at a crossroads. Maybe in this case Robin has something to teach Batman.

I am not suggesting that we create an American Passover holiday, or that we compose American prayers that are said every day, although it is certainly worth noting what that practice has done for Israel. It is only with the cultivation of such central founding ideas that a sense of shared purpose can be maintained. As it happens, there already is an American Passover of sorts: Thanksgiving. There already are American prayers of sorts: the Pledge of Allegiance and perhaps the preamble to the Constitution. Although the Pledge of Allegiance has fallen out of favor in recent years, it was a backbone of the educational system in past years. And while Thanksgiving is still celebrated, it has really lost any shared cultural meaning aside from being a time for family gatherings. The way to unite ourselves once again as Americans entails more than strategic political and internet reforms, and even more than a renewed commitment to and acceptance of the necessity that in order for the country as a whole to win, we ourselves as individual opinion holders cannot win every time. It requires us as a nation to cultivate once again common themes of which we are all proud. It requires that we all are able to once again stand together for the singing of the national anthem because we all believe in the ideals that it represents. Before further discussing this fraught issue, however, we must spend a moment considering truth, specifically our own country's historical truths, because it is these former truths which have recently come undone and which are negating this potentially strongest of unifying forces from saving and preserving our country, as it has Israel.

A BRIEF HISTORY OF TRUTH

In premodern times there were overarching truths which organized societies. For example, the Catholic Church had a monopoly on truth for many centuries throughout its areas of influence.

People knew the overall story of history and where they fit in through the narrative of the Church. This truth was very pervasive and quite strong, as evidenced by the trials of people like Galileo or Copernicus. In modern times, many of those older truths were overturned and replaced by newer truths. For example, many modern societies were organized around the principles of science and progress. It seemed to be a self-evident truth that science and progress would pave the way for the ultimate redemption of the human condition. Modern nation-states rose up to uphold truths about their identities and their specific cultures. The true purpose of America was therefore to defend the pursuit of life, liberty, and happiness. In France it was *liberte, egalite, fraternite*. This feeling of scientific and empirical truth was strong, inspiring, and simple. For example, journalism was simply about telling the truth. Science was about empirically figuring out the truth. If we just told the objective, scientific truth, everything could be figured out. By shining a light on all corners of society, reasonable people would clearly agree on the universal truths which would become evident, and the future course of society would almost chart itself.

In the postmodern era this conception of truth began to break down as people realized that the truth looks different depending on your biases and preconceived notions. Today, fewer and fewer people are so naive as to believe that the journalist's job is to report the truth. Rather, it is to sift through the facts and publicize those which comport with the story they are trying to tell (or sell, as the case may be). Thus we see many different news outlets reporting on the exact same story but portraying it in wildly different ways. America is the land of the free and the home of the brave. That is obvious and obviously true. Or is America the land of rampant and entrenched racism and thievery that stole every single thing of value it has amassed from either Native Americans or black Africans? God runs the world, has big plans for it, and has blessed our beloved country—"God bless America." That certainly is true—every American politician ends any speech of consequence with those very words. Or does God have no place in a modern society—rather, we use our own science and technology to solve all our problems, to conquer nature and disease and any other ills of the human condition? That's perhaps also true. Let's take Israel. Is Israel a modern miracle—the realization of a two-thousand-year-old dream to return a scattered people to their homeland? Or is it a colonialist enterprise to project westernism into the overwhelmingly Muslim Middle East—the last gasp of British, or perhaps now American, imperialism?

Obviously there are many ways to look at any issue; that is perhaps not news. But in the postmodern era, even foundational truths can no longer be trusted. We have learned from Einstein's concept of relativity that not only is space-time relative, but that even truth itself is relative. You can scrape away all the ulterior motives you want, try your best to dig down to the very bottom, to somehow get to the "actual" truth of an issue, but no matter how hard you try you can never get there. There is no bottom. There is just a never-ending pit of alternative realities. The best one can hope for is to disclose up front their biases as best they can, knowing full well that even the list of biases that they themselves generate is by definition incomplete because the generation of the list itself is based on their imperfect view of what constitutes bias in the first place.

How does one cope with such a situation? It is as if we are in a massive hall of mirrors with an unending array of truth versions. Do we just stick with the truths we were born into? If, for example, the Arab-Israeli conflict has two alternate truths, the Arab version and the Israeli version, do I just stick with the Israeli version because I happened to be born Jewish? Or do I delude myself into thinking that I myself can somehow sort it all out, arrive at some unperturbed truth all by myself? If there are two main alternatives, do I try to take some sort of average between the two—the truth of "moral equivalence" so common today in some news outlets? What happens when there are more than two truths, and there is no obvious way to arrive at any moral equivalence? If I can't even trust myself to arrive at the truth of a situation because I am self-aware enough to realize my own limitations, what then? Do I consciously try to realize my own biases and then purposefully apply a correction in the opposite direction, like many American Jews who seem to apply a correction to their "natural" affiliation with Israel to instead take the side of the Palestinian Arabs? Is that bad? Wrong? Does it arrive at a better, more calibrated truth?

It seems as if the universe has come unhinged, as if we've finally reached outer space and there is no longer any gravity to tell us which way is down and which way is up. We're all floating adrift, trying in vain to grab onto a piece of the spaceship for support, to orient ourselves somehow, and there is no longer any way to objectively identify "true truth." Already in 2005 comedian and political commentator Stephen Colbert coined the word "truthiness" to describe this phenomenon.[3] Is that really all we have left? Truthiness?

Getting back to America, it used to be that Americans felt America to be the new promised land, the new democratic "light unto the nations"[4] with a sacred mission to bring truth, justice, and the American way to the rest of the world. It used to be that America was the "last best hope of earth."[5] But these national principles have been torn down in recent years in the name of political correctness and historical revisionism.

I should point out that I am not denying that such historical revisionism doesn't have truth to it—obviously slavery and the catastrophes experienced by Native Americans and other minorities are true and need to be taught. But countries need their foundational mythologies. Those mythologies don't always need to be torn down just because they don't comport with historical events exactly. Their purpose is not to document the historical record, but to serve as reminders of who we want to be, of why we are here, and of what direction we want to go as we move forward. The fact that these national myths don't measure up to reality is not a reason to tear them down—on the contrary, it simply means there is more work to be done. We use those national myths not to look backwards to teach our history, but to light the way forward.

3. Zimmer, "On Language: Truthiness"; Colbert, "Colbert Report."

4. Isa 49:6, translation adapted from *Koren Tanakh, Magerman Edition.*

5. Lincoln, "Lincoln on America."

When those mythologies are conflated with history and therefore removed, cancelled, shunned, and forsaken, then the nation begins to come unglued and the way forward begins to splinter into a thousand separate paths.

A WIDER TRUTH

How has this unfolded in the recent past? There has been a movement in some quarters to promote a revisionist Thanksgiving history, to delete Thanksgiving altogether, or to change it into a day of sadness where we collectively plumb the depths of our guilt for the Native American genocide perpetrated by the early Americans. In a similar vein, protesters in Portland, Oregon in June of 2020 pulled down statues of Thomas Jefferson and George Washington. The following month protesters in Baltimore pulled down a statue of Christopher Columbus. Some might propose another example of this type of protest action is kneeling during the national anthem specifically in order to disrespect it, as a way of showing respect for African Americans, as if to promote the zero-sum idea that respecting African Americans and the American history of slavery cannot coexist at the same time as respect for America itself.

These acts share a common theme: that American history as commonly taught is incomplete and incorrect. This theme states that because American historical figures and events were not perfect but instead had flaws, sometimes egregious flaws such as owning slaves or displacing and killing the Native population, they can no longer be celebrated as American icons. While historically true, we must understand at a deeper level the purpose of those statues of Jefferson, Washington, and Columbus, and likewise the purpose of the Thanksgiving holiday. I am not suggesting that the sins of the past should be ignored, as some might prefer. The answer is not, as some polarized reactionaries would have it, to simply return to the old American history and iconography completely unchanged, or to lament a mythic past where we all were for God and country. But neither can we wholesale throw away our entire nation's founding ethos. We as a nation are experiencing an awakening where wounds of the past are becoming exposed. Perhaps it must be that early in this process, as people are swept up in the emotion of the moment, the best we can do is rage against the perceived old guard by toppling statues of our heroes, revising national holidays and willfully disrespecting our national anthem. But once the rage settles, if we wish to move forward together we must figure a way to retell our national story such that it speaks to us all. This must include the best ideals of our founding generation, but must also be widened to include the rectification of national sins such as slavery. National heroes such as Sojourner Truth, Frederick Douglass, Sitting Bull, and others can be added to our national mythology to form a more compete picture of what we stand for and how we have evolved.

HISTORICAL ACCURACY AND HEROES

How then are we to understand American heroes in light of the new focus on more accurate but often less favorable historical facts about them? The first thing to realize is that the hero we aspire to emulate and learn from in the present is never the same as the actual historical person in the past. This is not just an unfortunate result of our inability to understand true history; rather, it is a necessary and unavoidable part of what it means to have historical heroes in the first place. Because the amount of historical data about real people in the past approaches infinity, it is simply not possible to ever have a completely accurate picture of anybody in the past. How does this work? Consider the fact that the complete set of information about any past person would include, among other things, a complete record of everything single thing they ever said and every single thing they ever did, no matter how lofty or how mundane. Besides being physically unobtainable, the totality of this information would be too overwhelming to be intelligible. Information is only useful in so much as it tells a coherent story. Otherwise it degenerates into a random collection of disjointed facts. The argument, then, that the history previously told about, say, Thomas Jefferson or George Washington, was inaccurate, is a spurious argument. What is at stake is not the purported accuracy of the historical narrative but rather the selection of facts deemed important enough to be recalled and included in the narrative. We must also bear in mind that there is nothing which stipulates that this selection process must be static. Indeed, as society changes and matures it may be entirely appropriate to include new facts to form a more complete picture. But the key point is that when dealing with our national heroes, it is our responsibility as Americans to insist that whatever new story we create out of these new facts is one that fully comports with our highest aspirational ideals. Thus it may be completely reasonable to alter or update our understanding of our national heroes to include both positives to which we aspire and negatives we wish to avoid. This is, however, quite a different matter than simply tearing down wholesale our national heroes because they are not "accurate" or because a more accurate view reveals them to be real rather than perfect.

Looking at biblical stories, the founding stories of the successful nation of Israel, can serve as a guide. In those stories we see one important theme which is instructive for us today: the individual heroes of the Bible were never perfect—not a single one. Even Moses made mistakes. Both King David and his progenitor Judah failed grievously at different times in their lives, and both were honored with their positions of leadership not because of their ability to be perfect but because of their ability to recognize, repent, and grow from the depths of their failures. This theme holds not only for individuals but for the entire nation as well. The early nation of Israel also sustained grievous failures for which they were punished severely. But the success of a nation lies in its ability to recover from those mistakes and remain whole. It is therefore not anti-American for us to admit our national mistakes, but neither is it helpful for us to burn down the entire national project.

It is imperative that we continue to tell our national story together not by shifting the truth to an aggrieved party's alternative truth, but rather by widening the truth to encompass more. How does this occur in practice? School curricula may be a place to start, but the adult national ethos must be involved as well. Common national curricula centered around national holidays—Thanksgiving, Memorial Day, President's day, etc., might also be considered. Multiparty input from different groups of American stakeholders representing ethnic groups, religious groups, citizen groups, etc., can come together in local discussions, or using the now ubiquitous remote technology to which we are all accustomed, even nationally. This may seem like trivial pie-in-the-sky nonsense when compared to more commonly espoused recommendations such as political reforms, social media reforms, etc., however it is not. On the contrary, for an idea-based nation to succeed it must be able to tell a common story. The key point is not that the story must remain static, or even true to its founding ideals as some might say, but rather that when and if that story changes, that it remain inclusive enough to hold all the parts together. If different groups begin to tell separate stories, alternative truths, which do not speak to the rest of society, then no matter how many political reforms are made the country cannot long survive.

It would be nicer and easier if the solution to our divisiveness and polarization today could somehow ignore the thoughts of individual people and instead focus solely on systemic, structural reforms. It would be convenient if a few legal tweaks, some legislation, and a few regulatory changes would do the trick. After all, telling everyone to just think differently seems on the one hand too easy and on the other hand too difficult to succeed. But just as during the earlier discussion about medical guidelines becoming a crutch for independent thought, no matter what legal changes we make, without each individual citizen actively deciding to change the national culture in the ways we have described, the process simply cannot succeed.

SERVICE

Understanding our founding principles and cultivating a common narrative which can encompass all of our various tribes is an important step toward an American renewal. But the rediscovery and maintenance of our common national purpose cannot remain merely an idea if it is to continually reinvigorate future generations of Americans. In order for the idea to achieve permanence it must be embodied in action. Again, we can look to the longevity across a multitude of generations of the nation of Israel for guidance. The main prayer of the Jewish daily prayer service is the Amidah, a collection of nineteen brief prayers which is said individually and silently. It is recited while standing in the same position (facing the site of the ancient temple in Jerusalem while standing with the feet together) and has a distinctly meditative quality. The Amidah is also said on the Sabbath and on holidays although the middle section of prayers is different, altered to fit the theme of those days. A section of one of the prayers from the weekday Amidah reads as follows:

השיבנו אבינו לתורתך, וקרבנו מלכנו <u>לעבודתך</u>

Hashivenu avinu letoratecha vekarevenu malkenu <u>laʾavodatecha</u>

Return us, our Father, to your Torah, and bring us close, our king, to your <u>service.</u>

The following is from one of the prayers specific to the Sabbath Amidah:

וטהר ליבנו <u>לעבדך</u> באמת

Vetaher libbenu <u>le'ovdecha</u> be'emet

Purify our hearts to <u>serve</u> you in truth.[6]

You will note that although the Amidah prayers change depending on whether it is a weekday or the Sabbath, one word remains in common. That word is עבודה—*avodah*, which in the prayers is usually translated as "service" but actually has a more complicated meaning. More commonly it is translated as "work," as in going to a job to work, but in a more extreme form can also mean the work of

---

6. Translation of prayers is my own.

slavery. In a sort of middle-ground meaning, it can mean servitude or service, as in the work one performs in service of someone or something. The word itself is therefore neutral and can have either positive or negative connotations. It is the word used to describe both the slavery in ancient Egypt from which the ancient Hebrews were redeemed, as well as the service of God toward which they were enjoined at Mount Sinai.

As Bob Dylan once said, no matter what you do or your station in life, everybody's "gonna have to serve somebody."[7] We all do work. But that work can be positive or negative depending on its focus; depending on who or what master we "serve," as it were. As it pertains to our discussion, the very same work we all do, depending on its orientation, can serve to unite or to divide. Let's face it, as a nation deeply rooted in individualism, most of the work we do is focused on serving ourselves, as indeed it should be. We all need to take care of ourselves and our families first and foremost. But the focus of our self-work can function under the umbrella of a national sense of service. We can work to better ourselves and our families in service of the entire nation. In that way the two are not mutually exclusive.

The founding ideas we discussed earlier are just that—ideas. But service, or work, is action. The linkage of the two occurs when the ideas are embodied in action. In other words, the concrete actions of our lives must have a physical orientation toward the commonality of our founding ideas. President John F. Kennedy drew on this idea in his famous "ask not" speech. The phrase "what you can do for your country" is a direct appeal to this orientation of action in service of our common ideals.[8] Likewise, the terminology we use for work in the US military has a similar tone. We refer to "military service." When we thank veterans for their "service" we are not speaking merely of the physical work they did in their military unit. There are others who do hard physical labor as well but who are not in the military. What we are acknowledging with the

7. Dylan, "Gotta Serve Somebody."
8. Kennedy, "Inaugural Address," para. 32.

word "service" is the fact that their specific actions were oriented toward the common national good.

But if service is action, what does that kind of service actually mean? Are we saying that in order for the country to remain united, every single American must run out and enlist in the military? What did John F. Kennedy mean when he asked what you can do for your country? If we look to the modern country of Israel we see that one of its strongest unifying forces today is indeed the military, as military service is compulsory for two or three years after high school. In the early years of Israel's independence this was simply born out of necessity. However, with the passage of time this necessity has lessened. While most young Israelis today still engage in traditional military service, many do what is simply called "national service" instead of military service. This includes various national volunteer projects such as working in hospitals, nursing homes, schools, etc. Talk in the United States of requiring some type of national service has waxed and waned over the years but might be considered in this vein.

However, a culture of national service does not simply mean forced volunteer work between high school and college. It is also a state of mind. When I join a local church group, volunteer for a local politician, or engage in community organizing, am I doing it for the narrow interests of my own political party? Or am I doing it in service of the common good? Is the talk at the family dinner table about building up our own political interest group at the expense of others, or working to improve the nation as a whole? This is not to say that we must somehow expunge narrow political beliefs from our system. As discussed earlier in the section on shared decision-making, we must each pursue our own conception of what we feel is right for the country. But this focus on our own specific brand of politics must always be undergirded by a sense of national purpose.

One final quote from the same Jewish prayer, the Amidah, may be of interest. It is taken from one of the sections toward the end of the prayer which remains in common during the work week, the Sabbath, and holidays:

רצה יקוק אלוקינו בעמך ישראל ולתפלתם שעה, והשב את
<u>העבודה</u> לדביר ביתך

*Retzeh adonai eloheinu be'ammecha yisra'el velitfilla-
tam she'eh, vehashev et <u>ha'avodah</u> lidvir beitecha*

Be pleased, Lord, with your people Israel and heed their
prayer, and return the <u>service</u> of the temple.[9]

It is a plea to God to return the ancient Jewish temple service
which existed during the biblical first Jewish kingdom thousands
of years ago and the second Jewish commonwealth which existed
through the Persian, Greek, and Roman eras. The word used is
again the same, "עבודה—*avodah*—service." However, in this case
it doesn't refer metaphorically to serving God in general or serving our founding ideals, but rather to the specific temple service.
This can be understood in two different ways. First, it is a direct
linkage to the innermost focal point of the temple, its inner sanc-
tum, the holy of holies, the location of the ark of the covenant with
its golden cover and golden cherubs, which hearkens back to our
ideas of shared societal decision-making. But perhaps more importantly, the ancient temple service was a physical representation
of the national orientation of service.

The national orientation of service depends on the acts
of individuals. Each individual in the country physically acts in
ways specific to their own individual calling which support that
national framework. Thus there are myriad "micro-actions" which
compose that physical "service." However, the common national
symbol of that service and its embodiment in a real physical service reverberated throughout the entire population in the ancient
temple service, where the priests quite literally served God.

The temple has not existed in the nation of Israel for the past
two thousand years, yet the orientation of national service which
it represents has been memorialized in prayers such as this. Are
there physical representations in America today which can serve
as a reminder that we should all be acting in service of our unique

9. Translation of prayers is my own.

American founding ideals? Perhaps none as elaborate as the ancient Jewish temple service, but symbols need not be elaborate. (To be clear, the ancient Jewish temple in all its elaborateness has a much deeper and varied meaning than we are giving it in this brief discussion.) To give just two examples, I personally remember standing in class with my hand held over my heart while reciting the Pledge of Allegiance. I also remember gathering around the flagpole at summer camp to raise the American flag as we sang together the national anthem. I am sure you can think of many other such examples. These common physical acts are also a kind of physical representation of our national service, and are important as they ground us in a common national frame.

In summary, we must first understand the importance of common founding principles. Then we must craft a national mythology and narrative which can transmit these ideals inclusively to the many different tribes of our nation. Finally, we must concretize these ideals in a national culture of physical service in order to preserve the unity of our nation.

Chapter Four

Covenant

We can learn from Israel and Judaism through theories of shared decision-making, through the example of talmudic discussion, by maintaining the memory of founding ideas in the present consciousness of the nation, and in addition, through the biblical and ancient Israelite idea of covenant. As discussed previously, many people in America today feel they are American simply because that's where they grew up and that's where their family lives. There are many different groups and individuals living in America, each striving for their own piece of the American dream. Because they all share the same geographic space, they are forced to put up with each other. But the Israel of the Bible in its ideal form was and is more than that. It existed (and still exists) in a covenantal framework which obligated the people and their God to each other and therefore the individual people to one another. We Americans might benefit from utilizing a similar covenantal framework in the way we think about our country.

MARRIAGE AND THE CONSTITUTION

If you had to pick one document that serves as the basis for uniting our country it would probably be the Constitution. We commonly think of the Constitution as a legal document, basically a contract, that places obligations and restrictions on each state in the union, and through the states, on all American citizens. So how is this conception different than a biblical covenant?

A covenant does have some similarities to a contract. In antiquity, the Israelites agreed to keep the Torah (God's Law) and God agreed to protect the Israelites and be their God. However a covenant is more than a contract. Firstly, a covenant is meant to be eternal. Second, a covenant is meant to operate in all places at all times. Whereas a contractual relationship operates within defined limits both in time and space, a covenantal relationship operates continuously in all spheres of one's life. A prime example of this difference is that between a work contract and a marriage covenant. While the former places no claim upon me outside of work, the covenantal relationship of marriage is all encompassing. (To paraphrase Rav Mike Feuer, perhaps the converse would be easier to understand: If there were a place or time in your married life where you felt the need to remove your wedding ring, by all accounts this would indicate serious problems with your marriage.[1]) Finally, in a related point, a covenant is bonded with love. In fact, biblical Scripture speaks of the relationship between God and the Israelites metaphorically as the loving relationship between husband and wife. God loves the people of Israel, they love God, and the Torah is their marriage contract.

In one limited sense marriage is contractual. The husband and wife agree to do certain things for each other and abide by certain rules. The marriage "contract" places certain obligations and restrictions on the husband and wife in the same way that the Constitution places obligations and restrictions on each state in the union. But we intuitively know that marriage is much more than that. This is because in its ideal form it is the prime human example of a covenantal relationship.

In the Jewish tradition, all members of the nation of Israel share this covenant not only with God but with each other. In fact, two of the central Jewish commandments are exactly that: to "love

1. Rav Mike Feuer, personal communication via Zoom call.

the Lord thy God,"[2] and to "love thy neighbor as thyself."[3] The relationship of love thus extends between God and each individual, and also between and among all the individuals of the nation. Clearly as it might relate to America I am not suggesting that we all start to love the same God. However, if we take that covenantal framework and focus it inwards, toward each other, then we would all be bonded to each other and to our central founding ideas. But if love is a necessary condition for a covenant, how would that work in the case of America? Saying that Americans should just love each other might sound nice but practically seems like a utopian dream, too silly and juvenile to even be considered. Let us therefore explore this concept of covenantal love a bit further.

LOVE

In both Judaism and Christianity love is a very prominent concept. Both religions hold that one must love God and that one should love one's fellow human beings. But what does this really mean? The love with which we are most commonly familiar is that between husband and wife. Perhaps other common examples of modern love come from Hollywood, popular novels, and television shows. But in all of these cases the central feature of love is usually romantic, often with a not-so-subtle hint of sexuality. Other familiar types of love include that between parents and children, between siblings, or between best friends, none of which are built on romance. These different types of love bear little resemblance to each other on the surface. They have in common wishing good for the other partner such as success and happiness. The converse is also true whereby each partner wishes to prevent pain or sickness in the other and experiences empathy when such negative events occur. But a strict definition that fits all these various types is elusive. When we try to incorporate God into the covenantal love picture, any possible definition becomes even more strained. How can one

2. Deut 6:5. Translation is my own.

3. Lev 19:18. Translation is my own.

love an invisible and unknowable being? There can be no romance in such a relationship. Nor can we say we are worried about God's well-being or success, nor God's pain or sickness. What then does it mean, indeed what could it mean, to love God? Remember, we are looking for the common thread through all of these types of love: between husband and wife, between best friends, between parents and children, between siblings, and even between God and human beings. Also remember, we are not discussing this in order to convince you to love God (not that there's anything wrong with that . . .) but in order to understand the fundamental concepts about love as it relates to the covenantal framework which has successfully helped to sustain the nation of Israel over the past three thousand years, and in order that we in America might make use of similar concepts in our own national discourse. I would therefore propose that there are two distinct facets of this type of love which span all of these relationships. They are self-sacrifice and shared frames of reference.

SELF-SACRIFICE

Self-sacrifice does not mean merely that we are willing to pay for dinner for our partner, sacrificing some of our money for them. Rather, in its extreme form this means that we are willing to sacrifice our lives for our partner. A husband would surely be willing to die to save the life of his wife, and vice versa. Parents throughout time have been willing to die to save the lives of their children. Siblings or true best friends would similarly be willing to give up their life for the sake of their sibling or friend.

It is instructive to note that in Judaism, despite its central focus on the law, one is allowed to break any law in order to save a life. However, there are three specific cases in which upholding the law trumps even life itself. In those three cases one must be willing to give up one's own life rather than break the law. One case involves killing another person. If the situation were to arise, one must forfeit one's life rather than kill another. In other words, if someone puts a gun to your head and says, "You must kill so-and-so or else I'm going to kill you," according to Jewish biblical law you must say no, sacrificing your life for that of the other. That is because all members of the biblical nation of Israel were bonded to each other by a covenantal love relationship and therefore had to be willing to sacrifice themselves to protect one another. (That is not the only reason for this commandment, nor is it the only interpretation of its meaning. The most commonly cited reason for this commandment in the Talmud is that you have no right to decide whose life is more valuable—your own or that of another. But this alternate interpretation fits within the theoretical framework we are developing.)

What of the "love" relationship between the people and God according to the biblical narrative? It turns out that the second case where one must be willing to die rather than break the law involves exactly that; the public desecration of God's name. If someone puts a gun to your head and says, "You must publicly desecrate God's name or I'm going to kill you," according to Jewish biblical law you must refuse. Again, that is because if the Israelites shared a covenantal love relationship with God, they must be willing to die to "protect" God.

What is the third of the three cardinal cases where upholding the law trumps even life itself according to Jewish biblical law? In keeping with our discussion of self-sacrifice and covenant, it turns out that the third case involves exactly the third type of covenant we mentioned earlier—marriage. That is to say, the third instance where one must give up one's life in order to uphold the law involves sexual impropriety, commonly understood as committing adultery. According to Jewish biblical law one may not commit adultery and must be willing to give up one's life to uphold this law.

Thus the only three instances in the entirety of Jewish biblical law where one must be willing to give the ultimate sacrifice rather than transgress involve exactly and only the three types of covenantal love relationships we have described: the covenant between humans and God (we are commanded to love God, and therefore we must die before publicly blaspheming God), the covenant between all the members of the nation (we are commanded to love our neighbor as ourself, and therefore we must die before actively killing another), and the covenant between a husband and a wife (marriage partners love each other, and therefore one must die before committing adultery). This parallel between the legal code and the cardinal covenantal love relationships of marriage, God, and the collective individuals of the nation highlights the importance of self-sacrifice to the covenantal love relationship.

This is all perhaps biblically interesting, but is there a modern counterpart to this; something which remains operative in today's modern and secular society? Indeed there is: the military. Soldiers in the military are willing to die for people they have never met. Why? A cynic might say they are only doing it to protect themselves or their own families. Or that they are just adventure seekers who crave the adrenaline and violence of warfare. But in the truest and most noble sense, they are, as are all citizens of the nation, bonded to each of us in a covenantal love relationship and therefore are willing to sacrifice their lives in order to save ours. Thus we see that the first facet of covenantal love is that it requires self-sacrifice, and we have seen how it existed in biblical Israel both between God and the people, as well as between the people themselves.

FRAMES OF REFERENCE

Let us now turn to a discussion of frames of reference. In chapter 3 we discussed the elusive nature of truth in the postmodern world and we discussed how there are different frames of reference which each of us inhabit. We use these frames of reference to view the world and to view the events around us. Two people might therefore see the same set of facts and interpret them quite differently depending on their frames of reference. Republicans and Democrats for example both saw the same data early on in the COVID-19 pandemic and yet came to very different conclusions. Each group saw a very different truth in the same data set. This effect is so strong that if I were to discuss the COVID-19 pandemic with one of my friends who I knew to be a Republican, I might discuss it differently than I would with one of my Democrat friends.

There are just things I know the Republican would not believe or would not be willing to consider, which are different than those for the Democrat. When someone gives me their political opinion, how I listen changes if I know them to be a Democrat or a Republican. How often have you read an article and tried to figure out who the author was and what political affiliation they held prior to forming your opinion about the article, in order to help you categorize them as "on your side" or "on the other side?"

On the other hand, when my wife or best friend gives me advice, I know I can trust that advice because I know they are not pushing a certain agenda. I know they do not have any ulterior motives. I know that they only have my best interests at heart. What this means is that I know they share my frame of reference; that they see things the same way I do, or at least that they are able to inhabit my frame of reference honestly with me, and thereby give me real advice which is helpful to me and genuine. What this also means is that your wife, or your best friend, loves you. Part of love, the non-romantic part, a common thread through all the different varieties we have mentioned, is being able to inhabit the same frame of reference as your partner. In order to do that we must know them intimately, and in so doing we are able to see and understand their point of view; to see the world from their perspective.

But this poses a problem. Regarding the above example of Democrats and Republicans, does this logic imply that all Republicans love each other and all Democrats love each other simply because they share frames of reference about how they see the world? Perhaps, if self-sacrifice were added to the relationship and if these characteristics were seen to be exclusive or at least relatively much stronger for each individual group. But therein lies part of the problem. When we begin to create new covenantal relationships which supersede the overarching national one and which compete for strength and loyalty with the national covenant, minimally, we lose the power of covenant to unite us. Maximally, we may find the country actually splintering apart into warring subgroups.

This should not be understood to mean that you can only receive advice from people that love you. Therapists or psychologists give advice to their patients all the time, yet they do not love all their patients. But that relationship is a specific, transactional relationship. Technical advice would fall into the same transactional category. When one's computer is not working, one may seek advice from a computer expert. This is clearly not a love relationship. Rather, this is another example of a simple and specific transactional relationship. There exists a spectrum of overlap of frames of reference which two people, or indeed many people, can experience. When I ask advice from a computer technician on how to fix my broken computer, the technician must inhabit my frame of reference narrowly with respect to my computer problem in order to offer a successful solution. The technician must see the problem through my eyes if they are to really understand the problem. In that limited sense, we briefly share that frame of reference. We do not call that limited overlapping of reference frames love. (It may also be noted with respect to the previous discussion, that there is no expectation that the technician be willing to sacrifice their life for the sake of the customer or their computer.) When I as a doctor understand my patient's problems and see those problems through their eyes so that we develop a trusting relationship and I can offer them a successful diagnosis and treatment plan, we experience an overlapping frame of reference in the narrow context of the doctor-patient relationship. Yet we do not call that love.

The more familiar two people become with each other, however, the larger the area of overlap becomes between their two frames of reference. At some point, when the overlap is large enough—when it spans different subject areas, different times, and different spaces (and in conjunction with other features such as self-sacrifice as described above)—we begin to call the relationship love. The exact threshold where it becomes love is not a fixed line but is hazy, different for different people at different times. But one of the defining features of love relationships is that the two people who love each other inhabit the same frame of reference much of the time such that they understand "where the other person is coming from."

This becomes obvious in the medical field when dealing with the unfortunate case of sick individuals who are incapacitated and unable to make their own medical decisions. There is an entire legal code centered around this issue, but a common resolution is for either the spouse or the next of kin to make decisions on behalf of the incapacitated individual. This is because if those two people are bonded together in a love relationship, we assume that they know what each other would want. Why? Because they share similar frames of reference in the way they see the world. This is not to say that sharing the same frame of reference obligates the partners to agree with each other all the time. Mary Matalin and James Carville are a famous couple of opposite political persuasions who are happily married and presumably love each other.[4] Yet, despite their political differences they are able to inhabit each other's frame of reference honestly and thereby understand each other. Each knows that despite their political disagreements, the other wants what is best for them precisely because they are able to inhabit each other's reference frames both in politics and in the many other important areas of life.

One might be tempted to simply call this trust; to say that to love someone simply means you can trust them. While this may be partially correct, at a deeper level it is the ability to inhabit a common frame of reference which forms the basis for trust. Trust would be impossible if your partner could not inhabit your frame of reference. The only way you can trust somebody is if you are aware, even if only subconsciously, that they understand your truth, your perspective, your frame of reference.

This becomes even more apparent once we try to bring God into the picture, as was required by the original biblical conception of covenant. In a relationship which lacks any physicality, the only thing left (in addition to self-sacrifice) is to try to inhabit the same frame of reference. After all, what does it even mean to love God? Why are we supposed to do this? We are not planning to snuggle

4. Carville and Matalin, *All's Fair.*

on the couch, open a box of chocolates, and watch a movie with God. God certainly does not "need" our love because by definition God needs nothing. What therefore does it mean and what benefit could there possibly be from trying to somehow love God? Why would the Bible have mandated that the Israelites do something so seemingly strange and incongruous?

One way to understand love for God is that in loving God one knows that God can inhabit their exact frame of reference. One therefore knows that God truly has their best interests at heart, because God can see things as they see them and understands their point of view. Because they know that God can inhabit their frame of reference (indeed everyone's frame of reference), they know they can trust what God is telling them. In the law-based society of the Israelites, it was imperative to feel that way about God before following all of God's laws. Why else would anyone trust what God was saying? Would a Republican trust and blindly follow what a Democrat told them to do? (Perhaps not unless they were Mary Matalin and James Carville, and shared a covenantal love relationship.) In the context of the original biblical Israelite nation as construed in the Bible, the system would not work if nobody had any confidence that God was on their side. Further, because covenantal love is bidirectional, this also means that the people would strive to inhabit God's frame of reference, as it were, which in religious thought is held to be the ultimate and true frame of reference. While that is never actually knowable for human beings, through this covenant it becomes the object of our striving; the ideal frame of reference which we are trying to reach. When the Bible speaks about loving God, in addition to the self-sacrifice discussed earlier, part of that commandment speaks to the aspirational attempt to experience an area of overlapping frames of reference between human beings and God.

But why use the word love at all? Why not just say be nice to everyone? Does it not cheapen the word love to have it spread out so thin over such a wide area? Could the Bible not have said simply trust and be nice to everyone? To understand this we must put the two facets of the covenantal love relationship together.

Covenantal love occurs when both conditions are met; when we inhabit a shared frame of reference and when we are willing to sacrifice ourself for our covenantal partner. Again, human love can and often does involve much more than these two concepts, but when we look for the thread which is common to all forms of love—human to human and human to God—these are the two most salient facets.

Now that we have established the meaning of covenant and the meaning of the love necessary for such a covenant, let us return to the national stage. Does this mean that every person in Israel loved every other person equally? Clearly the answer is no. There are concentric circles of love. We love our spouse, our children, and our nuclear family the most. Then the circle expands to encompass our extended family and perhaps close friends, then our community, our city, our state, our country, and eventually all of humanity. But the national covenantal bond of which the Torah speaks is grounded in love and in a marriage metaphor. How can all people in an entire country share a relationship like that? We must remember that people can inhabit many different frames of reference, overlapping, at different points in their life and even at the same time with different people. When we speak of ourselves as being bonded together in a mutual national covenant, what then do we mean? Specifically, we mean three things: first, that we have contractual obligations to each other; second, that we share an ethos of self-sacrifice toward each other; and third, that we share a common frame of reference.

TEFILLIN

This may be a nice theory but is that all it is? Are these ideas, though intellectually interesting, nothing more than the scholastic cerebrations of philosophers and academics? Do these ideas actually find their way into the day-to-day practices of the members of Israel or Judaism? In fact they do, on a recurring daily basis. You may be familiar with the concept in Judaism of tefillin, sometimes called phylacteries. These are small black boxes which contain certain scriptural passages and are placed on the forehead and on the upper arm. They are secured in place with black leather straps around the head and wound around the arm and hand in a particular configuration. The tefillin are worn every day by observant Jews, usually in the morning during the morning prayer service. This practice has been maintained, uninterrupted, for over two thousand years. The scriptural passages contained in the tefillin and the binding of the tefillin on the arm and head are laden with meaning and numerous interpretations have been given through the ages as to their significance. Of particular interest to our discussion, however, is one aspect of this tradition. During the binding of the arm tefillin, after the black leather strap is wound around the forearm, it is wrapped specifically around the middle and ring fingers three times, as if to fashion a wedding ring out of the tefillin strap. As the strap is wrapped around the finger each of the three times, the following three part verses are recited from the prophet Hosea:

וארשתיך לי לעולם

וארשתיך לי בצדק ובמשפט ובחסד וברחמים

וארשתיך לי באמונה וידעת את יקוק

Ve'erastich li le'olam
Ve'erastich li betzedek uvemishpat uvechesed uverachamim
Ve'erastich li be'emunah, veyada'at et-adonai

And I will betroth you to me forever.
And I will betroth you to me with righteousness and with justice and with loving-kindness and with mercy.
And I will betroth you to me with faithfulness; And you shall know the Lord.[5]

The three iterations of the phrase "and I will betroth you to me" are recited with each of the three wraps of the tefillin strap around the finger as if to enumerate the specific marriage metaphor of covenantal love between the individual and God on a daily basis. This

---

5. Hos 2:21–22. Translation is my own. Hebrew from *Koren Tanakh, Magerman Edition.*

concrete daily action with the daily recitation of this passage serves as a constant reminder of the nature of the covenantal relationship.

Let us examine each of the three phrases in more detail to see how they map onto the framework we outlined earlier. The first phrase, "and I will betroth you to me forever," clearly maps onto the eternal time frame of the covenantal relationship. The first half of the second phrase, "and I will betroth you to me with righteousness and with justice," maps onto the contractual relationship of the covenant. Righteousness and justice are legal terms which refer to the contractual obligations of each party. The second half of that phrase, "and with loving-kindness and with mercy," maps onto the shared frame of reference theme discussed above. How so? Because when someone violates the law or breaks the justice aspect of the covenant, we can be merciful and forgive that person only when we are able to inhabit their frame of reference. When we can understand why they did what they did, seeing the situation from their perspective, we are able to create a space for change, growth, and improvement. Therefore, mercy implies a shared frame of reference.

The third iteration, "and I will betroth you to me with faithfulness," reflects the attribute of self-sacrifice. Sacrificing yourself for someone else is only possible with a deep-seated faith in that other person. While most of us will never be tested by having to sacrifice our life for our covenantal partners, the concept of faith does require another sacrifice of us. As will be described below, faith requires us to sacrifice some of our logic for the sake of our covenantal partners.

Thus we have seen how the three part phrase recited each and every day for thousands of years by observant Jews serves to reinforce the covenantal relationship they share with God and therefore with each other. But the third phrase about faithfulness alludes to one final point. Faith is the belief in something that cannot logically be proven. This shows how the covenantal love relationship must go beyond the realm of logic, political theory, and ironclad proof. While it is true that many of the reasons for such a national covenant can be elucidated, as we have done, and while it is true that one may indeed list the various arguments in favor of such an arrangement, at the end of the day if one is not willing to take a leap of faith the system will not survive. Logical arguments can easily devolve into simple lists of "what's in it for me?" The bonds between the people of a nation, as is true of the bond between husband and wife, cannot rest upon logic alone. Faith, the ability to go beyond reason, is an integral glue which cements the entire project together.

I am not suggesting that we in America form a new covenant with God. Modern America is a different country than ancient Israel or Judaism, first and foremost because of the separation of church and state. In the Israelite conception of national covenant, the covenantal bonds, including the love aspect of self-sacrifice and being able to inhabit common relational frames of reference, extended between God and the nation as a whole. Because each individual shared that same bond, they were all bonded to each other. We in America today might look to that model as a basis for our national covenant. If one were to downplay or eliminate the bond between God and the nation, you would be left with the covenantal bonds between individuals. That would be a good starting point for us here in America. Whether we should speak of a bond between the nation and God is an open question, but may not be necessary for the success of this approach. However, our nation is indeed steeped in unitarian religious imagery and rhetoric (clearly emanating from a basis of Christian theology, but with a conscious effort to remain unitarian given the separation of church and state), so that it would not be inconceivable to think about a covenant between a universal God and the United States, leaving the specific conception of God to each individual to decide for themselves, or to omit entirely as the case may be. I leave that as an open question.

MARTIN LUTHER KING JR.

What does this look like in practice? One exemplar with which you may be familiar is Martin Luther King Jr. He focused on our common national covenant as a way to unite all Americans rather than focusing more narrowly on specific racial identities. Jonathan Silver of the Tikvah Fund with guests Gerald McDermott and Derryck Green discuss in a podcast the fact that Martin Luther King Jr., as a Baptist minister, used to quote often from the Bible.[6] He and the Israelite prophets whom he liked to quote shared a common message: the Israelite prophets warned their nation how far they had strayed from the ideals of their founding covenant with God; Martin Luther King Jr. warned Americans in the 1960s how far they had strayed from their founding covenant—the American Constitution with its guarantee of equality. He sought not to castigate the oppressor but rather to raise up all Americans together using the language of our common covenant as expressed in the Constitution and in the Declaration of Independence.

To summarize and simplify things a bit, the ancient Israelites (and modern Jews) shared a covenantal relationship amongst themselves and with God. This relationship was based on a type of love which was applied to all people of the nation and to God. Rather than sex, romance, common interests, or hobbies, that type of love was manifested through the trust gained by inhabiting the same frame of reference and through self-sacrifice. Even without all the God-talk, the United States today could benefit from a similar covenantal framework by invoking an ethos of self-sacrifice and by actively cultivating a shared frame of reference in the way we see the world together. This overarching American frame of reference would be overlaid on the myriad other frames of reference which we individually inhabit. What this means practically is that, for example, progressive Democrats and pro-Trump Republicans, or even Black Lives Matter protesters and middle age white males susceptible to the false narrative of white supremacy, would consciously remember that despite their differences of opinion they still inhabit a common frame of reference stemming from their common, covenantal relationship.

One final point of interest may be learned from the Hebrew language spoken in the modern State of Israel. It is interesting to

6. McDermott et al., "Tikvah Podcast."

note that the modern Hebrew word for the Unites States is ארצות הברית—*Artzot Ha'Brit*. The word ארצות—*Artzot* means "Lands," or "States" in this case. But the word הברית—*Ha'Brit* does not mean "United." There is a specific word in Hebrew which means unity, and that is not the word used. The word הברית—*Ha'Brit* literally means "the Covenant." Modern Israelis call America quite literally "the Lands of the Covenant." Perhaps we can learn from our Hebrew name that, like biblical Israel, we Americans are bonded together by a covenant, all inhabiting a uniquely American frame of reference together. As such, we can trust that we all "have each other's backs." The biblical Israelites knew that an idea-based country needs active unifying forces to hold the country together. One we have already discussed is the unifying force of remembering founding ideas. The other is the unifying force of covenant. If it sustained the ancient Israelites and Judaism, perhaps it can sustain us in America today.

Conclusions

Telling Our Story

THE UNITED STATES HAS a massive problem of disunity. The country is polarized and hyper-partisan. While people have lamented the state of politics in this country since even before its founding, there does seem to be something qualitatively different with respect to recent events. Never before has there been a scene like the capitol riots at the close of the Trump presidency. Never before has there been so much open talk about splitting the country in two. While it is common to berate one's political enemy, only recently has either side begun to question the very legitimacy of the other side to exist at all. While this trajectory may be quite old, if left unchecked its ultimate destination can only be the eventual ruinous decay of our country. But if we do not understand the underlying basis of the problem we cannot hope to resolve it.

The biblical nation of Israel had the misfortune of being utterly destroyed and then being renewed seventy years later. When the Israelite exiles returned to their land, they mingled with local inhabitants who had migrated or been brought there in their absence. Rav Mike Feuer describes that part of the renewal of the nation at that time involved defining a story which would be common to the newly returning Israelites and exclusive of other non-Israelite tribes in the area. This meant defining the story itself as well as who was able to tell that story so as to keep it within a certain framework. If applied to America today this may sound exclusionary, as if we are saying that only a single story can be correct; the American story is this but not that. Part of our current problem is in fact exactly that. The country is splintering into rival groups, each of whom is trying to tell their own story about America which excludes the other. The correct response to this existential threat is covenant. One of the concrete ways that a covenantal relationship manifests itself among the citizens of a country, other than via some abstract sense of covenantal love and commitment, is through shared storytelling based on founding principles. We thus need to be able to tell our own American story. Like the ancient Israelites, our story must have some boundaries which define what is American and what is not. However, the story must be large enough to encompass all of our modern, evolving tribes.

The basic Lockean/Hobbesian notion whereby the function of the state is simply that of a mutual defense pact for self-protection so that each person can then be left alone and bothered as little as possible may be adequate as a minimalist proposition for the purpose of the state, however by itself may not be sufficient to overcome the divisive tendencies inherent to American society. After all, both Locke and Hobbes were English, and England, as we have discussed, has a long premodern historical identity based on geography, ethnicity, and a shared mythic-historic past, not to mention an actual monarchy to provide a degree of societal cohesion. Therefore the basic, bare-bones theories of those English political theorists may suit such a country without the need for any other glue to hold the country together. However in a much younger country such as the United States, one without such a shared historic identity, it is becoming ever more clear that such simple theories, although admirable and perhaps even necessary and correct, are insufficient for the long-term survival of the country. That missing link, the glue which holds the country together, is our covenant, manifested by the love we feel, the commitments we hold, and the stories we tell.

We must realize the importance of maintaining our own separate tribal identities within the covenantal framework. We must argue our own opinions honestly and forcefully, all the while admitting that none of us knows for certain what the Theoretically Better Decision (TBD) really is at any given moment. We must maintain an awareness that only together can we arrive at decisions which are as close as possible to the TBD. Although our political structures may not themselves be the root of the problem, we nevertheless should orient them in the right direction. We also must regulate our public platforms of discourse in support of that goal. We need to think for ourselves and honestly say what we think. We must be ever cognizant of the uniqueness and the fragility of the American experiment as an idea-based nation and should therefore look to the experience of biblical Israel and its inheritors, Judaism and modern Israel, for examples of how to sustain an experimental, idea-based society over millennia.

None of us know what is in store for this most unusual experiment called America. The natural tendency for many people is to bemoan the state of the union and to fall into a sad lament about how if only everyone else could just see things my way then we would all be united and we could put this silly bickering behind us. I hope that through the pages of this book I have brought to light some tools and perhaps some new understandings which can be used to reinvigorate our national project. Like most difficult projects, you get out what you put in. The easiest path, the one which does not require us to change ourselves at all, may be the continued path of resentment, mistrust, and anger currently on display all over our great nation. But it is often the more challenging path, the one which requires some degree of self-reflection, introspection, and nuanced understanding, which may actually lead us to a successful destination. Systemic structural changes can help, but a nation is nothing more than a collection of individual people. Each of us has to make the decision to change course if we are to change the course of the nation. It may seem that doing so would be swimming against the current. It may seem that nobody thinks the things I have outlined in this book. It may seem difficult for any one individual to chart a different course. But, in the words of Robert Frost, it is exactly taking the road less traveled which may just make all the difference.

> I shall be telling this with a sigh
> Somewhere ages and ages hence:
> Two roads diverged in a wood, and I—
> I took the one less traveled by,
> And that has made all the difference.[1]

1. Frost, "Road Not Taken."

Epilogue

THIS BOOK MAY BE a hard read for those who are politically opinionated. They may hear through the words of this book that their strongly held and carefully considered opinions, often a defining characteristic of their very sense of self, are being placed on some sort of random moral seesaw where they and their adversaries are given equal weight and the relationship between them is left to a kind of random chance. This despite the fact that their political adversaries are known by them to be wrong and in many instances unethical or even plainly evil. How can this be? How can it be that my correct, nice, and ethical opinions can be held up on an equal plane with those nasty, unethical, and downright evil opinions of the other side? And this business about hashing out our opinion, finding an Actual Path and acknowledging a Theoretically Better Decision (TBD) which sometimes is closer to my opinion and sometimes closer to that of my adversary may seem like no more than a ridiculous notion of arbitrary moral equivalence. It is as if we are being asked to retain some of our correct opinions while at the same time allowing a little bit of evil or nastiness from the other side just to appease them. How is this at all reasonable? After all, you don't negotiate with Darth Vader—you fight and hopefully eliminate him. You don't appease Darth Vader by saying, "Okay Darth, we'll allow you to kill just a few people with your force death grip and just a few planets with your Death Star superweapon so long as we can do our nice democratic thing generally most of the time." No, the only justifiable course of action is a fight to obliterate all traces of him and his evil minions.

While that may be true, one must realize that these are describing two totally separate scenarios. The "Vader scenario" versus the righteous and politically opinionated is a story about a correct opinion versus true evil. While it may be true that in such a case the evil must be vanquished, it is worth noting that within the story of the United States of America this would be equivalent to engaging quite literally in a civil war. That is a much different scenario than what I have been attempting to describe throughout this book. The scenario in this book is one where two sides are both striving to do what is right and just, and where each side respects and honors the other for doing so. If the two sides in this country are unable to see each other as legitimate in any way, then perhaps the game is already lost. Perhaps then we are truly victims of the aviation death spiral described in the very beginning of this book. We must therefore be clear-eyed and honest about which scenario we inhabit and which we wish to inhabit, the Vader scenario or the book scenario. However, a word of warning is perhaps in order about a certain creeping hypocrisy which can stealthily enter the minds of our politically astute citizenry. That is, a posture of professing to inhabit the second while acting as if we inhabit the first. Such a posture is not only hypocritical but will only serve to lock us into the same situation for the foreseeable future. For the sake of our country I sincerely hope this is not the case.

Bibliography

"America & Israel: Connected for Good." America Israel Public Affairs Committee. https://web.archive.org/web/20221230205358/https://www.aip ac.org/.

Carville, James, and Mary Matalin. *All's Fair: Love, War, and Running for President.* New York: Random House, 1994.

Churchill, Winston. "We Shall Fight on the Beaches." Speech, House of Commons of the United Kingdom, Jun 4, 1940. International Churchill Society. https://winstonchurchill.org/resources/speeches/1940-the-finest -hour/we-shall-fight-on-the-beaches/.

Colbert, Steven. "The Colbert Report: The Word—Truthiness." Comedy Central, Oct 17, 2005. https://www.cc.com/video/63ite2/the-colbert-report-the-word -truthiness.

Dylan, Bob. "Gotta Serve Somebody." Special Rider Music, Nov 1, 1979. The Official Bob Dylan Website. https://www.bobdylan.com/songs/gotta-serve -somebody/.

Fleischer, Richard, dir. *Fantastic Voyage.* Los Angeles: 20th Century Studios, 1966.

Frost, Robert. "The Road Not Taken." Robert Frost. Orig. pub. in *The Atlantic Monthly*, Aug 1915. https://www.robertfrost.org/the-road-not-taken.jsp.

Hirtenstein, Anna. "AMC, GameStop Swing as Meme Stocks Run Out of Air." *Wall Street Journal*, Jul 15, 2021. https://www.wsj.com/articles/amc-game stop-swoon-as-meme-stocks-run-out-of-air-11626354992.

Kennedy, John F. "Inaugural Address 1961." https://www.archives.gov/mile stone-documents/president-john-f-kennedys-inaugural-address.

The Koren Tanakh. Translated by Harold Fisch. Jerusalem: Koren, 2015.

Lincoln, Abraham. "Lincoln on America." National Park Service, Apr 10, 2015. https://www.nps.gov/liho/learn/historyculture/onamerica.htm.

McDermott, Green, et al. "The Tikvah Podcast: Gerald McDermott & Derryck Green on How Biblical Ideas Can Help Bridge America's Racial Divide." The Tikvah Fund, Feb 2, 2021. https://tikvahfund.org/library/podcast- gerald-mcdermott-derryck-green-on-how-biblical-ideas-can-help- bridge-americas-racial-divide/.

Niccol, Andrew, dir. *Gattica.* Culver City, CA: Columbia Pictures, 1997.

Bibliography

"Party Platform: The Democratic Platform" Democrats. https://democrats.org/where-we-stand/party-platform/.

"Republican Platform 2016." Republican National Committee. https://prod-cdn-static.gop.com/static/home/data/platform.pdf.

Schottenstein Edition Talmud Bavli. Rahway, NJ: ArtScroll Mesorah Publications, 1993.

Spielberg, Steven, dir. *Minority Report.* Los Angeles: 20th Century Studios, 2002.

———. dir. *Raiders of the Lost Ark.* Los Angeles: Paramount Pictures, 1981.

Tanakh: The Holy Scriptures. Lincoln, NE: Jewish Publication Society, 1985.

Zimmer, Ben. "On Language: Truthiness." *New York Times*, October 13, 2010.